REVEALING
KINGDOM
MYSTERIES

REVEALING KINGDOM MYSTERIES
NUGGETS THAT UNCOVER TRUTH

DR. JOHNNIE BLOUNT

BRIDGING THE GAP MINISTRIES

BRIDGING THE GAP

© 2023 Johnnie Blount
https://drjohnnieblount.com

All rights reserved. No part of this book may be reproduced, scanned, or distributed in any printed or electronic form without written permission from the author or Bridging the Gap Ministries.

Scriptures unmarked or marked KJV are from the KING JAMES VERSION (KJV): KING JAMES VERSION, public domain, unless otherwise noted as follows:

AMP: taken from the Amplified® Bible (AMP), Copyright © 2015 by The Lockman Foundation. Used by permission. lockman.org

ESV: taken from the ESV® Bible (The Holy Bible, English Standard Version®). ESV® Text Edition: 2016. Copyright © 2001 by Crossway, a publishing ministry of Good News Publishers. All rights reserved. Used by The Lockman Foundation.

GW: taken from GOD'S WORD®. © 1995, 2003, 2013, 2014, 2019, 2020 by God's Word to the Nations Mission Society. Used by permission.

ISV: taken from The Holy Bible: International Standard Version. Release 2.0, Build 2015.02.09. Copyright © 1995-2014 by ISV Foundation. ALL RIGHTS RESERVED INTERNATIONALLY. Used by permission of Davidson Press, LLC

NABRE: taken from the New American Bible with Revised New Testament and Revised Psalms © 1991, 1986, 1970 Confraternity of Christian Doctrine, Washington, D.C. and are used by permission of the copyright owner. All Rights Reserved.

NASB: taken from the NEW AMERICAN STANDARD (NAS): Scripture taken from the NEW AMERICAN STANDARD BIBLE®, copyright© 1960, 1962, 1963, 1968, 1971, 1972, 1973, 1975, 1977, 1995 by The Lockman Foundation. Used by permission.

NIV: taken from THE HOLY BIBLE, NEW INTERNATIONAL VERSION®, NIV® Copyright © 1973, 1978, 1984, 2011 by Biblica, Inc.® Used by permission. All rights reserved worldwide.

NKJV: taken from the NEW KING JAMES VERSION (NKJV): Scripture taken from the NEW KING JAMES VERSION®. Copyright© 1982 by Thomas Nelson, Inc. Used by permission. All rights reserved.

NLT: taken from the HOLY BIBLE, NEW LIVING TRANSLATION (NLT): Scriptures taken from the HOLY BIBLE, NEW LIVING TRANSLATION, Copyright© 1996, 2004, 2007 by Tyndale House Foundation. Used by permission of Tyndale House Publishers, Inc., Carol Stream, Illinois 60188. All rights reserved.

RSV: taken from Revised Standard Version of the Bible, copyright © 1946, 1952, and 1971 by the Division of Christian Education of the National Council of the Churches of Christ in the United States of America. Used by permission. All rights reserved.

TMB: taken from THE MESSAGE. Copyright © 1993, 1994, 1995, 1996, 2000, 2001, 2002. Used by permission of NavPress Publishing Group.

ISBN: 978-0-9899888-5-8

PRINTED IN THE UNITED STATES OF AMERICA
10 9 8 7 6 5 4 3 2 1

For all those Saints who hunger and thirst for the Kingdom.

ACKNOWLEDGMENTS

*Blessed be the God and Father of our Lord Jesus Christ,
who has blessed us with every spiritual blessing
in the heavenly places in Christ.*

Ephesians 1:3 NKJV

As I look at the blessings in my life and see the people who surround me, I feel my heart swell with gratitude.

I want to thank my beautiful wife, Donnis, my partner in life and in ministry. She is truly a blessing and an inspiration as we journey through life together.

I'm grateful for my children and their families and the pure joy my grandchildren give me.

And I want to acknowledge and thank the Bridging the Gap ministry team and all those who support us in so many ways. May the Lord bless and prosper them in every aspect of their lives.

Johnnie Blount

CONTENTS

1. Abba's Love 1
2. Identity 19
3. Agape Love 31
4. Authority of the Believer.......................................49
5. Kingdom Principles 71
6. Led by the Spirit 101
7. The Power of the Word.. 115
8. Purpose 135

About the Author 151

1

ABBA FATHER'S LOVE
He First Loved Us

We love Him because He first loved us.

1 JOHN 4:19

> *For God so loved the world,*
> *that he gave his only begotten Son,*
> *that whosoever believeth in him should not perish,*
> *but have everlasting life.*
>
> JOHN 3:16 KJV

My friends, many times I think about the attitude we have toward the Father, how we wonder whether or not He loves us. How can we not know that He loves us when John 3:16 tells us that God so loved the world that He gave His only begotten Son? This verse says a lot more than what we just read.

Jesus became our propitiation. *Propitiation* is a two-part act that involves appeasing the wrath of an offended person and being reconciled to him. The Father gave the gift. He did not offend us—we offended Him. He loved us so much that He provided the gift for us, a gift that would soothe and appease Him for our wrongdoing. This atonement was good for the sins committed before the cross and for those after the cross.

The key to all of this is 2 Corinthians 5:19-21, which tells us that the Father Himself was in Christ when He came to reconcile the world back unto Himself. Son!

Be the Word!

No matter what we've done or failed to do,
the Father's love has washed away our sins.

*Blessed be the God and Father of our Lord Jesus Christ,
who has blessed us with every spiritual blessing
in the heavenly places in Christ, just as He chose us in Him
before the foundation of the world,
that we would be holy and blameless before Him.*

Ephesians 1:3-4 NASB

When we spend time meditating on the Word, we can see how much the Father really loves us. To understand the love of the Father will help us clean up doubt, fear, and unbelief. All of these come from not understanding how much we are loved.

Paul's letter to the Ephesians talks about how the Father adopted us to and for Himself to show us His kindness and mercy. We are not accustomed to love and kindness unless we earn it.

To know that the Father commanded His love toward us while we were yet lost and did not know Him is a game changer.

Be the Word!

*Anything we desire in faith is already a given
because of the Father's love.*

> *See what love the Father has given us,*
> *that we should be called children of God;*
> *and so we are.*
>
> 1 John 3:1 RSV

John 3:16 says the Father loves us enough that He gave us His only begotten Son, not only to give us eternal life with Himself, but to give us the opportunity to become His children. His desire is to adopt us as His sons and daughters.

This is His perfect will so we can be heirs of all His promises and have abundant life—not only in the life to come, but also in the now. He wants us to walk in the fullness and abundance of life today.

I know that we do not comprehend the magnitude of His love for us. Friends, if we did understand this, we would not walk in fear, worry, or stress. We would have peace because we would trust His Word. We need only to use our imagination and ask ourselves what we would do for our children.

Be the Word!

> *The Father's perfect love casts out*
> *all our concerns, distress, and uncertainty.*

There is no fear in love [dread does not exist], but full-grown (complete, perfect) love turns fear out of doors and expels every trace of terror! For fear brings with it the thought of punishment, and [so] he who is afraid has not reached the full maturity of love [is not yet grown into love's complete perfection].

1 JOHN 4:18 AMP

I do not yet fully understand true love. It is beyond human comprehension.

We need to ask the Holy Spirit to give us revelation of what love truly is. This is why John said, "Behold what manner of love the Father has bestowed upon us."

I am fully convinced that when we have revelation of love and realize how much our Father loves us and that He is love and nothing but love, then we will release every care, want, or need into His hands.

Be the Word!

*When we've got God, we've got Love.
And when we've got Love, we've got it all!*

> *In this the love of God was made manifest among us,*
> *that God sent his only Son into the world,*
> *so that we might live through him.*
>
> 1 JOHN 4:9 RSV

The Father sacrificed His only Son for us. He did not need to do that; He did it because He loves us so much. Why then is it so hard for us to believe that the Father will grant us anything else we want? Everything is already paid for by His Son with His death. So, we must realize we are valuable to the Father. He proved that because He was willing to sacrifice what He loved the most, His only Son.

We struggle to believe that anyone can love us that much because we do not know our self-worth. We must spend time with and in the Word and speak and meditate on the Word so we can believe it. We must become indoctrinated into the Kingdom by the Word of God. That revelation of love will transform our lives for eternity.

Be the Word!

The Father paid the highest price for us.

> *Love bears all things, believes all things,*
> *hopes all things, endures all things.*
> *Love never ends ...*
>
> 1 Corinthians 13:7-8 ESV

It strains my brain when I try to imagine what love really is. When we look at the definition of love according to the Bible, we can see that only God can truly love humanity.

The church and the world are filled with all different kinds of people with all different personalities, all different problems, from all walks of life. Sometimes it seems as if some are on medication, others need to be on medication, and some forgot to take their medication.

When we contemplate in the natural that Jesus died to redeem this mess of humanity, we have to agree that only the Father has what it takes to love us.

My friends, this tells me that since our heavenly Father loves us enough to die for us, then we can be assured He has already taken care of whatever troubles we face.

Be the Word!

The language of the Kingdom of God is love.

*You know that you were ransomed from the futile ways
inherited from your fathers, not with perishable things
such as silver or gold, but with the precious blood of Christ,
like that of a lamb without blemish or spot.*

1 Peter 1:18-19 RSV

Sometimes you can love a person so much it makes your heart throb. There is nothing you wouldn't do for that person. They could ask you for the world, and if it were in your power, you'd give it to them.

That's the way the Father feels about us. There is nothing He hasn't given us. We must understand how much He loves us. We must believe that He loves us and receive His love.

Once we receive His love, then we know there is no sickness, disease, depression, or loneliness that can hold us captive because we understand that our Daddy has already given us the answer to all things. That answer is the love and sacrifice of His Son, Jesus, who paid the price for us to be free from all demonic forces.

Be the Word!

There's no limit to the Father's love for us.

Love is patient, love is kind. It does not envy, it does not boast, it is not proud. It does not dishonor others, it is not self-seeking, it is not easily angered, it keeps no record of wrongs. Love does not delight in evil but rejoices with the truth. It always protects, always trusts, always hopes, always perseveres. Love never fails.

1 Corinthians 13:4-8 NIV

When I read 1 Corinthians 13—which tells us what love really is—I'm astounded. I realize this kind of love can truly come only from heaven.

To be able to love is a gift from the Father, and we know the highest expression of that gift was and is His only begotten Son, Jesus.

Jesus expressed His love for us by taking thirty-nine stripes and having the flesh ripped from His body. He could have stopped because of the pain and agony. He could have stopped when they plucked the beard from His face, put the crown of thorns on His head to mock Him, when they slapped Him or spit in His face. But His love was greater than the pain He endured.

That love was for you. The Word says that Jesus endured shame on the cross because of the love He had for us.

Be the Word!

Love is the greatest force in the world.

> *For He rescued us from the domain of darkness,*
> *and transferred us to the kingdom of His beloved Son.*
>
> COLOSSIANS 1:13 NASB

It is very important for us to understand that we don't have to be afraid of our future. Our Father has drawn us unto Himself.

As parents, we always want our children to have the very best. We will do our best for them even when it requires a sacrifice from us.

We must understand that our Father loves us so much that He came to the earth Himself in Christ Jesus to redeem us back unto Himself. The Word tells us that our Father adopted us unto Himself through Christ Jesus (Eph. 1:5).

Religion wants you to see Him as an angry God rather than a Father. He is not angry with us. He poured out His wrath on Jesus Christ at the cross for us. Our goal should be to gain a better relationship with the Father. He is a good Father.

Be the Word!

Because we have a good Father, we have a great future.

*... in whom we have redemption through his blood,
even the forgiveness of sins.*

Colossians 1:14 KJV

Saints, when we take a look at the Word and we believe and receive the Word to be true in our life, then we can stand with confidence and know our heavenly Father loves us so much that He gave His only Son to perish on our behalf.

Not only did Jesus die for us, but the Word says He went to hell on our behalf. He took a beating of thirty-nine stripes and was bruised for our iniquity so we would not have to endure what He endured for us.

When you understand the love of the Father, it is easy to lay your head upon His bosom and know that everything you're going through is already complete. It is finished. He has given us victory, healing, and prosperity.

We must receive this by speaking the Word to ourselves and meditating on it daily. This is how much He loves us.

Be the Word!

*We can have confidence in the Word when we know
how much our heavenly Father loves us.*

If ye then, being evil, know how to give good gifts unto your children: how much more shall your heavenly Father give the Holy Spirit to them that ask him?

Luke 11:13 KJV

When we look at the death and resurrection of our Lord and Savior, Jesus Christ, we can see the passion and love the Father has for the world—so much that He was willing to take His best and sacrifice Him for mankind.

We can see love through the action of the Father and the Son on our behalf. The Word tells us that God is love. This is a love we cannot comprehend.

When we understand how much we love our children and think about what sacrifices we would make to bless them with a better life, we know there is no limit to our love.

So we should have the confidence that when we pray, God our Father hears us. Because of His love for us, we can know that what we ask for is assured if we don't cast away our confidence.

Be the Word!

We can trust the Father to give us good gifts!

> *The life which I now live in the flesh*
> *I live by the faith of the Son of God,*
> *who loved me, and gave himself for me.*
>
> GALATIANS 2:20 KJV

When I was a child, I knew that Jesus was born at Christmas, but I didn't know that He died on the cross or rose from the dead. I remember hiding eggs for Easter and getting new clothes. Mama would tell us it was bad luck to wear new clothes to church on Easter, so we would wear them to the tobacco farm and back, and then they were worn so we could be legal to wear them to church.

I had no understanding of how much the Father loved me until I was thirteen and learned about the resurrection of Jesus Christ. I sat and cried that someone took the pain of three nails in His hands and feet. That sounded terribly painful, but the scary part was knowing that someone physically died for me.

Then and there, I made a decision to live for Jesus because He died for me. I wanted to please Him because I had never known true love, and that experience changed my life forever.

Be the Word!

Love caused Jesus to give His life for us;
love should cause us to live our life for Him.

> *There is no fear in love, but perfect love drives out fear*
> *because fear has to do with punishment,*
> *and so one who fears is not yet perfect in love.*
>
> 1 John 4:18 NABRE

When we understand this, we will no longer be afraid of our heavenly Father. We can believe we are healed because of the stripes Jesus took for us. We will believe the Word, which tells us that when we repent He blots out and doesn't remember our sins of the past. The only way He knows about those sins is when we put Him in remembrance of what we did.

When we understand the love of the Father, we will no longer hold the image of the angry God of the Old Testament that religion wants us to believe about our Father.

Saints, now we must spend time with the Father in the Word, encouraging ourselves, meditating on the Word, praying in the Spirit, and making daily confessions over our families, our country, and our own lives.

Be the Word!

Get to know the Father Who loves you.

For God was in Christ, reconciling the world to himself, no longer counting people's sins against them. And he gave us this wonderful message of reconciliation.

2 Corinthians 5:19 NLT

As a child, I saw God the Father as an angry God waiting to hurt or judge me for things I had done wrong. I didn't understand that His purpose was to deliver me from condemnation and damnation, to bring me into the light, righteousness, and holiness, and to bring me to the knowledge that I am His son and He is my Father.

As a parent, I understand that a good, godly father will give his resources, even his life, for his child. This is what our Father did for us on the cross of Calvary.

My friends, if Daddy loves us this much, then all we need to do is to believe and receive His Word.

Be the Word!

Everything the Father did for us, He did because He is love.

*And I will be a father to you,
and you shall be sons and daughters to me,
says the Lord Almighty.*

2 Corinthians 6:18 NABRE

My son Thomas was born very prematurely and with multiple health challenges. He was so small I held him, not in my arms, but in my hand. My heart just ached and hurt, and I cried out with love, wishing I could take his place and carry the pain for him. I wanted so badly to help him.

Even with that experience, I cannot begin to comprehend the Father's thoughts when He looked upon suffering humanity and wanted to call us His sons and daughters. What love!

Our Father did not stand by, helpless. He put His love into action and took our place before we were born into this world. He paid the price for us to be His sons and daughters. Now, we must receive His love and believe and trust His Word.

Be the Word!

*Our Father, the Creator of the universe,
chose us to be His sons and daughters.*

Happy is he who has the God of Jacob for his help,
whose hope is in the Lord his God,
Who made heaven and earth, the sea, and all that is in them;
Who keeps truth forever,
Who executes justice for the oppressed,
Who gives food to the hungry.
The Lord gives freedom to the prisoners.
The Lord opens the eyes of the blind;
the Lord raises those who are bowed down;
the Lord loves the righteous.
The Lord watches over the strangers;
He relieves the fatherless and the widow;
but the way of the wicked He turns upside down.

PSALMS 146:5-9 NKJV

Saints, I really don't need to say anything else. The Lord did all this for them in the Old Testament when He was just their Lord. Now, He is our Father, and we are His children.

We can have that blessed assurance that we are in good hands with God Almighty as our Father.

Be the Word!

We have a Father who loves us more than we can ever imagine.

2

IDENTITY
A New Creation in Christ

*Therefore, if anyone is in Christ,
he is a new creation;
old things have passed away;
behold, all things have become new.*

2 Corinthians 5:17 NKJV

> *What is man, that thou art mindful of him?*
> *and the son of man, that thou visitest him?*
> *For thou hast made him a little lower than the angels,*
> *and hast crowned him with glory and honour.*
>
> PSALMS 8:4-5 KJV

What is man? Why does God love man so much that He called Himself our Father? Psalms 82:6 says that man is the child of the Most High. Now, that is a statement.

The Word tells us that God is not satisfied with just being our Lord. The Lord Almighty Himself says that man is His house and He walks with man, and we shall be His people. He will be a Father unto man, and we will be His sons and daughters (2 Cor. 6:16-18).

Can you begin to understand why the Word tells us not to worry and to fear not, because our heavenly Father has chosen us to be His sons and daughters? How much more could we ask than to know that the Creator of the universe Himself has chosen man?

Be the Word!

If the Father is for us,
what mountain can stand against us?

IDENTITY

[We are writing] about the Word of Life [in] Him Who existed from the beginning, Whom we have heard, Whom we have seen with our [own] eyes, Whom we have gazed upon [for ourselves] and have touched with our [own] hands.

1 JOHN 1:1 AMP

In this verse, John is telling us that he didn't read about Jesus—he saw Him, touched Him, walked, talked, and ate with Him. He was there at the funeral when Jesus raised the widow's dead son. He watched Jesus put mud on the blind man's eyes and heard Jesus tell the man to go and wash at the pool of Siloam.

John is saying he still remembers when Jesus walked on the water and the disciples were frightened because they thought He was a ghost. Jesus told them to be at peace, that it was He. Peter said, "If this is you, Lord, bid me to come." John witnessed Peter and the Master walking on the water together.

That same Jesus Who was with them in the flesh now dwells within us!

Be the Word!

We are the witnesses of today.
We are the temples of the Living God.

> *Now if we are children, then we are heirs—heirs of God and co-heirs with Christ, if indeed we share in his sufferings in order that we may also share in his glory.*
>
> Romans 8:17 NIV

It is exciting to know we have eternal life with the Father, and it's also exciting to know that eternal life begins for us the day that we receive Jesus Christ as our Lord and Savior.

Saints, when I look at all the great patriarchs of the Old Testament and read about the things they accomplished here in the earth without Jesus Christ, and some even without the Word of God, I cannot help but think how much more we should be able to do.

We have Jesus abiding in and with us. We have the power of the Word itself dwelling within us. We have the Holy Spirit in us. If that is not enough, we share the same Father as Jesus Christ.

In His Word, He told us we shall be His sons and daughters and that He will be our Father. Now, that's mind boggling and life changing to think that the God of the universe is our Father.

Be the Word!

Our Father owns everything we see and cannot see, and we are His heirs.

Identity

For we are the temple of the living God; as God said: "I will live with them and move among them, and I will be their God and they shall be my people."

2 Corinthians 6:16 NABRE

My friends, do you ever take time to think about the Scripture that tells us we are the temple of the Living God? Son! That is a mystery that only the Holy Spirit can reveal to us. Our carnal minds cannot begin to comprehend who or what we are in and for the Kingdom of God.

We are the house of the Father, the Son, and the Holy Spirit. As Jesus was the Living Word who walked the earth, so also are we.

We must learn how to release the glory, the power, and the anointing of the Holy Spirit Who abides inside of us.

We have all of the Godhead dwelling within us. This is why the enemy works so hard to rob us of our identity as he did Adam and Eve. The serpent told Eve, "If you eat this fruit, then you will be like God." Yet she was already made in the image and likeness of God. It is imperative that we know who we are.

Be the Word!

As Jesus was the Living Word Who walked the earth, so are we.

> *What harmony can there be between Christ and the devil?*
> *How can a believer be a partner with an unbeliever? And what*
> *union can there be between God's temple and idols?*
> *For we are the temple of the living God.*
>
> 2 Corinthians 6:15-16 NLT

It overwhelms me to think we are the house of the living God. This means that He dwells within us and walks in us and with us. The Word tells us we are His sons and daughters. That is hard for our natural minds to comprehend.

The reason the enemy is so angry at us is because we are made in the image and likeness of our Father. Satan is jealous of who and what we are.

I could cry when I look at the Word of the Father that calls us to come out and be separated from unbelievers. We are a "holy people set apart."

Saints, we have overcome because the Father is with us and for us.

Be the Word!

> *There is no place I'd rather be*
> *than in the love of our heavenly Father.*

For as many as are led by the Spirit of God, these are sons of God.

Romans 8:14 NKJV

My friends, it is very important to understand that we are sons of God. (Yes, if men can be the bride of Christ, women can be sons.) The reason the Word tells us about being led by the Spirit of God is that most believers are carnal-minded Christians. They walk by, are controlled by, and try to make godly decisions out of their emotions.

The Word tells us that a carnal mind is hostile to the Spirit of God. So, when the Holy Spirit tells you something, your mind will go against what the Holy Spirit said every time because the mind does not know the things of God. The carnal mind is in agreement with the natural, not the supernatural.

You can never check with your mind to assess your level of faith. The Word tells us to walk by the invisible rather than by the visible.

Be the Word!

When you walk by faith, you are confident of the victory rather than fearful of the storm.

For we are His workmanship [His own master work, a work of art], created in Christ Jesus [reborn from above—spiritually transformed, renewed, ready to be used] for good works, which God prepared [for us] beforehand [taking paths which He set], so that we would walk in them [living the good life which He prearranged and made ready for us].

Ephesians 2:10 AMP

This verse will cause you to grow new hair. Paul tells us that we are God's masterpiece and we have been recreated in Christ Jesus.

The Father has prearranged and ordained us beforehand and set us aside just for Himself to do a great work in our generation and time. This is our generation and our time to make a mark on the earth.

We need to seek the face of the Father to get clarity today about what He wants us to do, so we can be in step with His plans for our life and for those He has called us to serve.

Be the Word!

You are no longer the same person you were when you were born into this world.

Identity

But the Helper, the Holy Spirit whom the Father will send in My name, He will teach you all things, and remind you of all that I said to you.

John 14:26 NASB

If we truly believe the Word, then there should be a difference between us and people who do not know Christ. The world and religious people should know that there is something about us that is different from them.

Why are we different? The Holy Spirit is our teacher—and that's higher education indeed!

God the Father has made Jesus to be our wisdom and knowledge. Since we have His wisdom and knowledge, we should be a head above all those we work with and go to school with and live around. Most of the time, we are busy trying to blend in with everyone else.

We are not called to blend in, but to lead.

Be the Word!

Who is your teacher and who are you listening to?

But it is from Him that you are in Christ Jesus, who became to us wisdom from God [revealing His plan of salvation], and righteousness [making us acceptable to God], and sanctification [making us holy and setting us apart for God], and redemption [providing our ransom from the penalty for sin].

1 Corinthians 1:30 AMP

When we look at the Word, we can see that we are missing some revelation of who we really are in Christ Jesus. The Word tells us we are righteous and are already in right standing with the Father, the Son, and the Holy Spirit.

If we would let the Holy Spirit teach us, we would have so much more peace and rest in our lives. The Holy Spirit leads us into all truth.

Many times we allow religion and culture to lead us, guide us, and give us our self-worth. The Word tells us that we are in this world but are not a part of this world. The world does not know Christ nor understand His ways because the things of the Spirit must be revealed by the Spirit. Saints, we must train our spirit to listen to the Holy Spirit and follow what He tells us to do or not to do.

Be the Word!

The Holy Spirit who abides in us is the most intelligent person of all.

And if the Spirit of him who raised Jesus from the dead is living in you, he who raised Christ from the dead will also give life to your mortal bodies because of his Spirit who lives in you.

Romans 8:11 NIV

My friends, it is a magnificent thing to know that we have God in the form of the Holy Spirit within our human flesh. Why be afraid of today or tomorrow? Why be afraid about whether we live in this world or live in heaven?

It is important for us to understand that we have the power of the Holy Spirit in us. We must learn to yield to Him so He can do supernatural things through us on the earth. Remember, the Holy Spirit can do only what we yield to Him to do. If we do not submit to the Holy Spirit, then He can't do what the Father wants done on the earth.

Fear competes with the Holy Spirit. It comes to stop us from being free to obey the Father. You have wealth, wisdom, creative ideas, and peace in the time of trouble within you. The same force (the Holy Spirit) that raised Christ from the dead dwells in our flesh.

Be the Word!

*When you look in the mirror,
you see the house of the Holy Spirit.*

3

AGAPE LOVE
Love One Another

*I give you a new commandment:
love one another.
As I have loved you,
so you also should love one another.*

John 13:34 NABRE

> *If I speak in the tongues of men and of angels, but have not love, I am a noisy gong or a clanging cymbal.*
>
> 1 Corinthians 13:1 RSV

So many times I see the body of Christ going to church, reading Bibles, praying, prophesying, and speaking and praying in tongues, all of which are good. I recommend we do all these things and then some. We talk about how much we love the Father and express what He has done for us and tell each other we will serve and worship Him all the days of our lives—also good.

But all that is in vain if we don't love one another. Apostle Paul said even if we give all of our goods to take care of the poor and do not have love, we gain nothing.

How can we love God when we neglect to love the people He lives in? Remember, what we do for others we do unto Him.

Be the Word!

When you love God, you will love man.

> *Just as the Father has loved Me,*
> *I have also loved you;*
> *abide in My love.*
>
> JOHN 15:9 NKJV

Since the Father loves us and has forgiven us, then we should love and forgive others. Jesus said the world knows that we are His disciples by the love we have one for another, not by how many scriptures we can quote, how long we can pray in tongues, or how many likes we have on Facebook or Twitter. The size of your church or ministry means nothing without love.

When you have love, it shows. Kingdom is love. Religion is lip service. Religion performs in the light to be seen by man. Kingdom operates in secret. It does not need human affirmation, because Kingdom and love are inseparable.

When you understand the Kingdom, you will begin to serve others.

Be the Word!

The love we show to one another tells the story of how we abide in Jesus and His love abides in us.

> *Love is patient and kind; love is not jealous or boastful;*
> *it is not arrogant or rude. Love does not insist on its own way;*
> *it is not irritable or resentful; it does not rejoice at wrong,*
> *but rejoices in the right. Love bears all things, believes all things,*
> *hopes all things, endures all things.*
> *Love never ends.*
>
> 1 CORINTHIANS 13:4-8 RSV

This verse comes from the mother of all chapters. Here, Paul teaches about love or charity. He helps us to understand what love looks like and how love is supposed to act. I have been walking with the Lord for over forty years, and I can always see how I need to improve in love.

It is a full-time commitment to learn how to love and how to be loved.

Sometimes we're afraid to love because we're afraid of being hurt, but the Word tells us that perfect love casts out fear. We can become unloving and unlovable because of our past hurts and failures. What we must understand is that everyone has been hurt, and we have all hurt each other. What we must do is ask the Holy Spirit to teach us how to love and forgive, and how to let go of offenses.

Be the Word!

When you succumb to fear, you give place to the devil.

> *Greater love has no one than this,*
> *than to lay down one's life for his friends.*
>
> JOHN 15:13 NKJV

Many times we have no problem laying down our lives for the Lord, but when it comes to laying down our lives for each other, we have issues because of differences we have had with someone in the past.

Paul tells us that love does not hang on to grudges (1 Cor. 13).

My friends, we know it is easy to love people who love us, and it is easy to treat people kindly who treat us kindly. However, there are times it takes the love of the Father to be able to love our family or church family.

Yet, the world knows we are different when they see the love of the Father operating through us. We have love in us because we have the Father in us. The Word tells us that the Father is love. 1 John 4:8 states "He that loveth not knoweth not God, for God is love."

Be the Word!

When you have God in your heart, you have love.
And when you have love in your heart, you have God.

Even if I dole out all that I have [to the poor in providing] food, and if I surrender my body to be burned or in order that I may glory, but have not love (God's love in me), I gain nothing.

1 Corinthians 13:3 AMP

Good works are not enough. Taking care of the poor out of duty is not enough. People need love. Even the Father Himself loves to be loved and loves to love. Because we are made in the likeness and image of our heavenly Father, it is in our nature to reach out to care for others who are different from us.

If it weren't for the love of the Father, where would we be?

We need to give what we desire to have in our own personal lives. We want to be loved; therefore, we must give love. If we love others, we can change the world we live in.

Be the Word!

To truly love our heavenly Father, we must love people.

Agape Love

Love is large in being passionate about life
and relentlessly patient in bearing the offenses
and injuries of others with kindness.
Love is completely content and strives for nothing.
Love has no desire to make others feel inferior
and has no need to sing its own praises.

1 Corinthians 13:4 TMB

My friends, when I read this, I feel convicted. How many excuses do we find every day not to love? We need to get out of our comfort zones when we're dealing with people, serving, traveling, and encountering people who are not very nice.

Lord, help me.

Only the Father can teach us what love is and what it looks like. It is never about living for ourselves. It is always about loving and serving Him in others.

Saints, let us love one another.

Be the Word!

It takes self-sacrifice to demonstrate agape love.

> *Love is predictable and does not behave out of character. Love is not ambitious. Love is not spiteful and gets no mileage out of another's mistakes; it bears no record of wrongs!*
>
> 1 CORINTHIANS 13:5 TMB

When I read this verse I understand that only the Lord can help us to love each other, our family, and enemies like this. How many times have we wished revenge upon people who have hurt us? How many times have we rejoiced within ourselves when we have heard about negative things happening to those with whom we have had difficulty?

Our greatest desire needs to be love. We need to seek the Holy Spirit daily to help us keep 1 Corinthians 13 in mind. This chapter will bring satisfaction, peace, and harmony to so many people if we learn to walk in it.

Be the Word!

*We can gauge our love for the Father
by how much we love others.*

> *Love sees no joy in injustice.*
> *Love's delight is in everything that truth celebrates.*
>
> Corinthians 13:6 TMB

It should pull at our conscience to think how guilty we have been to rejoice when we see things happen to those who have mistreated others or even us. But love does not rejoice over others' misfortunes. This Word should cause us to search ourselves to the core.

I want to be the first to confess my need for the Holy Spirit to teach me and help me to love—not just with words or emotion, but with that agape love that the Father has already put within our spirit.

Jesus said there is no greater love than this: that a man lay down his life for another. That is what we are supposed to do in the Kingdom.

Be the Word!

> *The love of God in our hearts*
> *causes us to be the light of the world.*

Love is a fortress where everyone feels protected rather than exposed! Love's persuasion is persistent! Love believes. Love never loses hope and always remains constant in contradiction.

1 Corinthians 13:7 TMB

We can see the Father written all over this verse. Being in the Kingdom, we recognize the love the Father has bestowed upon us over our lifetime. During the times that we were guilty, we were yet loved and not exposed.

A fortress is a place of protection. That is what love is. So, we must ask ourselves, are we walking in love? Are we giving to others what we desire others to give back to us?

When people can see the body of Christ demonstrating the love of the Father, they will have that longing in their hearts to be a part of God's family in the Kingdom.

Be the Word!

*Those who sacrifice to give love to others
are a magnet that draws love to themselves.*

Prophecy and speaking in unknown languages and special knowledge will become useless. But love will last forever!"

1 Corinthians 8:8 NLT

Love is a word that I cannot adequately define. It is so powerful, yet the world thinks that it's weak. We know that it takes strength to be able to do good unto someone who mistreats you and to be able to love them as though they have never done you wrong.

Love is something that comes from the heart, not from emotions, because emotions are fickle. They come and go. Love is the Father, and He is eternal. We all need love like a fish needs water.

The Word says we reap what we sow. Do not neglect to give away that which you desire. Jesus said there is no greater love than for a person to give their life for a friend.

Be the Word!

God's sons and daughters need to demonstrate His love now more than ever before.

Love never fails [never fades out or becomes obsolete or comes to an end]. As for prophecy (the gift of interpreting the divine will and purpose), it will be fulfilled and pass away; as for tongues, they will be destroyed and cease; as for knowledge, it will pass away [it will lose its value and be superseded by truth].

1 Corinthians 13:8 AMP

We admire the prophets God uses as His mouthpiece and those who have great insight in the things of God and sometimes wish we could be like them, but the greatest of these things is love.

We have the Spirit of the Father, which is the Spirit of Love, dwelling within us. We must cultivate love. We must aim to love people because everything else we admire and long for will pass away. The one thing we know is that the Father is for eternity.

Be the Word!

We cannot have love without having the Father.

When I was a child, I spoke and thought and reasoned as a child. But when I grew up, I put away childish things.

1 Corinthians 13:11 NLT

When we look at racism, we can see that many in the world are walking in darkness and do not know love because their father is the father of darkness. Jesus said that satan was a liar and a murderer from the beginning.

When we come into the Kingdom and the Light, we can understand why Paul said he set aside childish things. Mature Christians who understand the heart of the Father cannot exclude anyone from the Father's love.

We see the body of Christ in the church fighting over and being divided on Sunday mornings by racism. True love never cares about the color of a person's skin. True love recognizes we are born from the same Father, and His love is unconditional.

Be the Word!

*When you look at the sunset,
you can see that heaven is made up of all colors.*

And be not conformed to this world: but be ye transformed by the renewing of your mind, that ye may prove what is that good, and acceptable, and perfect, will of God.

Romans 12:2 KJV

It hurts my heart to see racism, denominationalism, and division in the body of Christ as it is in the world. We must remember that we are different from the world. We must sacrifice our feelings and do the right thing to each other and even to our enemies.

Jesus said anyone can love someone who loves them, but it takes the Spirit of God to help us love someone who hates us.

Love always conquers fear, hate, pain, and darkness. There is no greater force in the universe than love. Plants, animals, and people respond to love.

Jesus said there is no greater love in this life than a person who lays down his life for a friend (John 15:13). That is strong love. Let us show the world what real love looks like.

Be the Word!

Love cannot be legislated. It comes from the Father.

> *If anyone boasts, "I love God," and goes right on hating his brother or sister, thinking nothing of it, he is a liar. If he won't love the person he can see, how can he love the God he can't see? The command we have from Christ is blunt: Loving God includes loving people. You've got to love both.*
>
> 1 John 4:20 TMB

When I think about how the world sees racism everywhere, it bothers my mind and my heart. It is amazing how we focus on the few hate-mongers, the few bad preachers, politicians, policemen, teachers, and then paint the whole world in that light.

Do you ever look at flowers? There are so many different colors, shapes and purposes in the world. God loves variety, not just one kind of flower or one kind of bird. It is the same with people.

How can you think you are going to heaven when you hate another because of the color of his skin? The Lord made every human. Not one person was created by satan. The Lord is the one who gives life. Every race, nationality, and culture of people is put here for the Lord's pleasure.

Be the Word!

Because the Father loves variety in everything, including people, we should too.

Thanks be to God for His indescribable gift!

2 Corinthians 9:15 NASB

My friends, one of the greatest celebrations of the year is the birth of our Lord and Savior, Jesus, the Messiah. This is a great season for us to express the love of the Father. It's a time when people's hearts seem to be more open. So we need to take this opportunity to share the love of the Father by blessing them with gifts.

Remember, we are here to help each other to get home. Once upon a time we all were lost and someone took the time to express the love of the Father to us.

Whether it's Christmastime or not, ask the Holy Spirit to give you someone to reach out to. The Holy Spirit will give you the right things to say and will prick their hearts to receive His love. If you will minister to the outward man, the Holy Spirit will minister to the inward man.

Give someone the greatest gift of all, Jesus and eternal life (John 3:16).

Be the Word!

*At Christmastime and throughout the year,
we can surely say to mankind, "Joy to the world!"*

If someone says, "I love God," and hates his brother, he is a liar; for he who does not love his brother whom he has seen, how can he love God whom he has not seen?

1 John 4:20 NKJV

Fellow believers often try to tell me how deep they are in the Word. The number one way they can test themselves is to examine their love. Many Christians profess to love Jesus, the Father, and the Holy Spirit. But how we can say we love God whom we have never seen, and yet despise or dislike our Christian brothers in the body of Christ whom we do see?

Paul wrote that men will be lovers of themselves and that selfishness is the root of all sin. He went on to warn us against holding on to the appearance of being religious without living Jesus' commandment of love (2 Tim. 3:5).

My friends, some brethren are easier to love than others. I can testify to that. But we must ask the Holy Spirit to help us love those we struggle to love. This is what sets us apart from the world: the love we have for one another.

What is in your heart?

Be the Word!

Love is expressed not only in words but in actions.

4

AUTHORITY OF THE BELIEVER
Christ in Us

*"Truly, truly I say to you,
the one who believes in Me,
the works that I do, he will do also;
and greater works than these he will do;
because I am going to the Father."*

John 14:12 NASB

> *Believe in the Lord Jesus, and you will be saved—*
> *you and your household.*
>
> ACTS 16:31 NIV

When you are going to release the Holy Spirit intentionally, you must set the atmosphere to bring people to expect results in agreement with the Holy Spirit, the Word, and you.

I remember having a healing service in Carmi, Illinois. We told the people what was going to happen. We shared testimonies about the other times we saw the power of God manifested. We set the expectation for the Holy Spirit to act.

On the third day, when they came up for prayer, people got healed. Their teeth were filled with enamel, silver, and gold. Some people in the basement were healed also. Others had family members at home who got healed when we didn't even pray for them.

Be the Word!

The power within you only works when you release it.

"But you will receive power when the Holy Spirit comes on you; and you will be my witnesses in Jerusalem, and in all Judea and Samaria, and to the ends of the earth."

Acts 1:8 NIV

We say that we believe the Word, but if we do, then we need to have a greater desire for the Holy Spirit to manifest Himself in and through us. We are the people with the power, so there should be a noticeable difference between us who are Spirit filled and led and those who are not.

Jesus calls us to be a witness to Him to the ends of the earth. Being a witness means that our family, neighbors, co-workers, and schoolmates can see the anointing of the Lord upon our lives.

We must focus to be more conscious of the power that is in and with us. When trouble comes, the world needs to know where to find help because they have seen the witness of your life. They should know that the Lord is with you by what they have seen you overcome.

The same Spirit that raised Jesus Christ from the dead dwells in us!

Be the Word!

Remember, greater is He that is in us than he that is in the world.

> *You know ... how God anointed Jesus of Nazareth with the Holy Spirit and power, and how he went around doing good and healing all who were under the power of the devil, because God was with him.*
>
> Acts 10:37-38 NIV

We tend to forget that we are the temple of the Holy Spirit. Sometimes we try to send the Holy Spirit to go do this or that for us, but unless we go, He can't go, because we are His voice, hands, and feet. The Spirit of God travels with and in us.

Jesus had to *go* in order for the people to be healed. We think we just have to sit at home and pray. Just as the Father used Jesus to *go* to heal the sick and oppressed, He needs to do the same today in and through us.

Saints, we must go, as Jesus said, into all the earth.

Be the Word!

Don't be like the world, be the Word!

> *The Son is the radiance of God's glory*
> *and the exact representation of his being,*
> *sustaining all things by his powerful word.*
>
> HEBREWS 1:3 NIV

The Greek for *word* in this verse is *rhema* and means *the spoken word, an utterance*. All creation is sustained by God's utterance of His word. When He speaks, He releases His *dunamis* or miraculous power and ability that create what He speaks. If He had not spoken His Word, then nothing would exist.

Let me remind you that we are created in His image and likeness (Gen. 1:26). The definition of *image* is *resemblance or similar in appearance* and the definition of *likeness* is *manner*, which means a way of doing or being. This tells me that we not only look similar to our Father's image, but we have the same mannerisms, ability, and being or existence (Acts 7:28).

In Psalms 82:6 God tells us, "I have said, ye are gods; and all of you are children of the most High."

When we can grasp what that truly means, we will manifest the abilities and privileges that belong to us.

Be the Word!

We are who He says we are,
and we can do what He says we can do.

> *Then God said, "Let Us (Father, Son, Holy Spirit) make man in Our image, according to Our likeness [not physical, but a spiritual personality and moral likeness]; and let them have complete authority over the fish of the sea, the birds of the air, the cattle, and over the entire earth, and over everything that creeps and crawls on the earth."*
>
> Genesis 1:26 AMP

God gave man dominion (reign, rule, prevail against, and overtake) over the earth and every living thing in it. This is why Adam had to name the animals, because he was in charge of the earth.

Ephesians 6:12 tells us we need to reign in the spiritual world in order to change the natural world. When Jesus entered into the earth realm as a man, He came into the earth to redeem man back to the Father and restore the dominion that Adam lost in the garden.

This is why Jesus was able to speak to trees, storms, sickness, and demons, and they submitted to Him. He understood that Father God had given dominion in the earth to man.

Be the Word!

You have God-given authority and dominion here on the earth.

And God blessed them, and God said unto them, "Be fruitful and multiply, and replenish the earth, and subdue it; and have dominion over the fish of the sea, and over the fowl of the air, and over every living thing that moveth upon the earth."

Genesis 1:28 NKJV

When God created man and placed him on the earth, He did not give him religion or denominations. He gave him dominion (control, authority) on the earth.

This is why Jesus always spoke to sickness and commanded it to leave. He understood that Adam was the god-man in the earth before he committed betrayal with the serpent and lost dominion over the earth to satan. This is why the Word calls satan the god of this world.

The reason Jesus came into the earth was to take back dominion and redeem man back to his rightful place. Jesus is a good example. He didn't pray for the problems (mountains) to be gone. Instead, He took His authority and spoke. This is what we are supposed to do also.

Jesus said, "Behold, I give unto you power to tread on serpents and scorpions, and over all the power of the enemy: and nothing shall by any means hurt you" (Luke 10:19).

Be the Word!

Speak to your mountain; don't just talk about it.

> *"You nullify the word of God in favor of your tradition that you have handed on. And you do many such things."*
>
> Mark 7:13 NABRE

Many times believers go for weeks, months, or even years without seeing their prayers fulfilled. That is because religion and the traditions of men have caused the Word of God to have no effect in their lives.

Our traditions or beliefs cancel the will or the Word of God. The Father cannot work outside of His Word. If we cannot believe the Word, then it cannot work because of our unbelief. The Word only works through faith.

At times we pray and ask the Father for something that already exists, but because we cannot see it in the natural realm, we do not receive it. Therefore we continue to suffer the consequences of unanswered prayers.

We are made in the likeness of our Father (God) with the ability to create. Our mind or imagination and the words of our mouth create.

Be the Word!

We must be able to imagine it and speak it in order to have it.

God said: Let there be ... and so it happened.

GENESIS 1 NABRE

In Genesis 1, God said let us make man in our image and likeness. Man was in God's imagination first and then He spoke that He would create man. Not until He imagined and spoke in Genesis 1 did He produce Adam in Genesis 2:7.

What's in your imagination must be spoken first. After you speak it, then it will come forth. We must speak into existence our dreams for our home, finances, and healing.

In order to do this, we must have the understanding that we are made in the likeness of God, which means we have the ability to imagine, speak, and then produce just as our Father does.

In Genesis 11, the people decided to build a city and a tower that would reach heaven. The Lord came down to see it and had to stop them because He said nothing would restrain them from doing that which they had imagined to do (Gen. 11:6). That is how powerful our imagination is.

Be the Word!

What can you imagine and speak forth?

And You have made them a kingdom (royal race) and priests to our God, and they shall reign [as kings] over the earth!

Revelation 5:10 AMP

Saints, we talk about Christians having authority every week and almost every day. Psalms 82:6 states, "I said, 'You are gods, And all of you are sons of the Most High.'"

God has given us dominion in the earth and over the earth. He wants us to rule the earth and take dominion over the spiritual realm. He wants us to use our faith to speak things into existence so we can have a healthy, prosperous, and successful life.

As kings, we have rule over the natural realm, and as priests we have spiritual authority. So when we speak the Word, heaven agrees with us, and what we say comes to pass.

Be the Word!

When you can see yourself as a king, you will recognize the authority you have in the earth.

> *The Son of God appeared for this purpose,*
> *to destroy the works of the devil.*
>
> 1 JOHN 5:8 NASB

Jesus has destroyed the works of the devil. Now, the only thing the devil has left is a voice. He lies, deceives, and accuses us to bring us to fear and agree with him. If we submit to him, then we submit to his lies and receive them into our lives.

All we need to do when he tries to lure us in with his tactics is to fight the good fight of faith. Just as Jesus used the Word to resist him and cause him to flee, we must use the Word to resist him, and he will flee from us. This is the victory Jesus has won for us.

James 4:7 says when we submit to God and resist the devil he will flee. To submit to God, who is the Word, we must acknowledge the Word to be supreme by trusting it to work when we speak it. When we speak the Word, its power goes to work on our behalf, and because it is light which dispels darkness, the devil has to flee.

Be the Word!

We must use the Word to resist the devil,
and he will flee from us.

And his gifts were that some should be apostles, some prophets, some evangelists, some pastors and teachers.

Ephesians 4:11 RSV

Jesus became flesh and blood. When His body lay in the tomb for three days, His Spirit went into the lower parts of the earth to redeem man back unto the Father. In Hebrews, it says that He took back the power and authority from satan.

When He ascended, He set the captives free and left gifts to the body of Christ. Those gifts are the five-fold ministry of apostles, prophets, pastors, evangelists, and teachers.

The reason we don't see the supernatural manifest in churches today is because we have done away with the five-fold ministry and have not received the gifts of the Holy Spirit given to us on the day of Pentecost with the evidence of speaking in tongues.

Be the Word!

*The Son did not come to help angels;
He came to help the descendants of Abraham.*

> *And He put all things [in every realm] in subjection under Christ's feet, and appointed Him as [supreme and authoritative] head over all things in the church.*
>
> EPHESIANS 1:22 AMP

We have been programmed by religion and the culture we live in, and that makes it diffcult to comprehend the authority we have through Christ's victory. We do not grasp that we have authority over satan and his works. We don't recognize that the enemy is under our feet.

Saints, I don't like to say this, but we are our own enemy. Hosea 4:6 plainly tells us that Christians are destroyed because of the lack of knowledge. James said that our tongue poisons our whole body. Not the enemy's tongue, but our tongue. We know that poison will cause us to be sick and sometimes even bring us to death.

Because of religion, we think we are fighting satan; but the Word says that Jesus came into the earth to destroy satan's works (1 John 3:8). Satan is already defeated. It is our tongue that will either make us or break us.

Be the Word!

If we can only remember, the enemy is already under our feet.

> *The Lord is my light and my salvation;*
> *Whom shall I fear?*
> *The Lord is the strength of my life;*
> *Of whom shall I be afraid?*
>
> PSALMS 27 NKJV

This psalm came to life for me one morning at school when I was meditating on the negative report the doctor had given me. He said I had an incurable disease. Fear gripped me to the point I had a hard time finding sleep. The Lord spoke to me in this Scripture, and my life has never been the same.

Once you understand who the Lord is in your life, then fear begins to lose its grip on your imagination and your health, because now you know there is nothing in this life that is more powerful than the Lord Himself.

Everything that was made, both seen and unseen—including all power and all authority—was created by Him. So, we do not have to be afraid of a lie in any situation or circumstance that may occur in our life. We have the Word of truth and that truth makes us free.

Be the Word!

Fear cannot stand up to the Word of God.

> *And I will give you the keys of the kingdom of heaven, and whatever you bind on earth will be bound in heaven, and whatever you loose on earth will be loosed in heaven.*
>
> Matthew 16:19 NKJV

Jesus said to Peter, "I shall give you the keys to the Kingdom." What do you think that means? Then He went on to say, "Whatever you permit on the earth, heaven will permit." Why did He say that? He said it because man has dominion over the earth.

Heaven cannot intervene in the earth realm unless we invite God in through prayer, and then the prayer is not good if we ask God to do what He has already given us authority or dominion over.

We pray and ask Jesus to remove our mountains when Jesus plainly told us if we shall speak to the mountain, then it will obey us—not God, Jesus, the Holy Spirit, or angels. It will obey *us* because we have dominion over the earth.

When the Lord created the earth, it came forth by the words He spoke. The invisible became visible.

Be the Word!

When you have dominion, you have authority and power to speak, and what you speak to shall obey you.

> *And the Lord said to Moses, "Why do you cry to Me? Tell the children of Israel to go forward. But lift up your rod, and stretch out your hand over the sea and divide it.*
>
> Exodus 14:15-31 NKJV

The Lord made man in His likeness and image and gave him dominion over the earth. We read this, but it does not become our reality until we have to walk in it.

When Moses stood at the Red Sea, he prayed, and the Lord asked him why he was talking to Him. He asked Moses what he had in his hand, and Moses answered that he just had a rod. The Lord told him to stretch forth the rod. When Moses did that, the wind began to divide the sea. When Moses used the rod, it worked for him.

Too often, we talk to the Lord and ask Him to do what we ourselves can do. He has already given us all that we need. When we use what God has given us, it will work for us also.

What do you have in your mind, mouth, or hands? Stretch it forth and see what the Lord will do.

Be the Word!

What has God put in your hand to bring you success?

> *God said, Let Us [Father, Son, and Holy Spirit]*
> *make mankind in Our image, after Our likeness,*
> *and let them have complete authority.*
>
> GENESIS 1:26 AMP

My friends, what do you think it means for the Lord to give man complete authority over the earth? If *you* have authority over your home, then *I* don't have authority over your home or over your health, finances, joy, or peace.

It is important for us to understand that unless we use our authority, we will live in poverty, sickness, lack, and so many other things that we don't want to live in. It is imperative for us to comprehend that because Genesis 1 says the Lord gave man complete authority.

This means the Lord does not have authority over your situation. You must take your authority and loosen that which needs to be loosened and bind that which needs to be bound in your life by using your mouth, tongue, your thoughts (meditation) to call into existence what you want.

Be the Word!

The key to the Kingdom of God
is to use your God-given authority.

> *"I will give you the keys (authority) of the kingdom of heaven; and whatever you bind [forbid, declare to be improper and unlawful] on earth will have [already] been bound in heaven, and whatever you loose [permit, declare lawful] on earth will have [already] been loosed in heaven."*
>
> MATTHEW 16:19 AMP

I believe when we get to heaven we will be so disappointed to know all the good things we could have had here on earth if we had read and believed the Bible and done exactly what it said.

The Word tells us that we have authority over our salvation and whether we receive the Holy Spirit or not. We can choose to walk in health or in sickness.

Jesus is saying that when we take authority over something on the earth according to the Word of God, heaven will align itself with us. Heaven will bring to pass what we speak out of our mouths if it agrees with the Word of God.

Be the Word!

Wise words bring many benefits (Prov. 12:14 NLT).

Do you not discern and understand that you [the whole church at Corinth] are God's temple (His sanctuary), and that God's Spirit has His permanent dwelling in you [to be at home in you, collectively as a church and also individually]?

1 CORINTHIANS 3:16 AMP

My friends, the Word says, "He who has ears to hear, let him hear." You may need to read this verse again to help you understand that no sickness, disease, or any other demonic power that has risen against you can stand because the Word says that you are the church.

The power of the Holy Spirit dwells in us. What a mystery and revelation when Paul said that Christ, the hope of glory, abides inside of us. There is no greater force in the universe than the force that is living with us and in us.

Be the Word!

Only Jesus has the words of life.

> *Whatever you imprison, God will imprison.*
> *And whatever you set free; God will set free.*
>
> MATTHEW 16:19 GW

Saints, it amazes me to think who we are and what we are in the Kingdom of God. We do not yet know or comprehend who or what we are in this world. We are kings and priests as Jesus, our elder brother, was.

What have you set free today? A better question might be what have you imprisoned today?

When we look at our salvation with the eyes of religion or denomination, we do not comprehend the magnitude of the authority we have in this world. My friends, it is mind boggling to think that heaven waits for us to take dominion over our situations and circumstances.

Paul said if the Father is for us, then it doesn't matter who or what sickness or disease may be against us.

Be the Word!

If we can comprehend the magnitude of our authority, we can change our world.

> *Jesus answered them, "Is it not written in your law,*
> *'I said, you are gods'?"*
>
> JOHN 10:34 NASB

Adam was the god of the earth, and the Lord is the God of the universe.

This helps us understand what happened when God asked Ezekiel if the dry bones could live and then told him to speak life to the bones. Ezekiel prophesied to the bones and told them what the Lord told him to say. When the God of the universe spoke to the bones, nothing happened, but when Ezekiel spoke to them, they came together.

Jesus said to Peter, "I will give you the keys of the kingdom of heaven. Whatever you imprison, God will imprison. And whatever you set free, God will set free" (Matt. 16:19).

My friends, we need to ask ourselves what we are doing daily with our keys to the Kingdom.

Be the Word!

Only those who do the Father's will
can enter into the Kingdom.

5

KINGDOM PRINCIPLES
Here, Now, Within You

*Jesus answered them,
"To you it has been granted to know
the mysteries of the kingdom of heaven,
but to them it has not been granted."*

Matthew 13:11 NASB1995

> *Jesus Christ is the same yesterday, today, and forever.*
>
> Hebrews 13:8 NKJV

When you don't understand that the Kingdom means a finished work, you spend your time trying to get the blessings of the Lord to work in your life. When you understand, you know that if what you desire aligns with God's Word, it is already complete. Then it makes sense that Jesus said when you pray you are to believe and receive.

Religion has us wait on the Father to answer our prayer and trust that He is going to come through on His Word, when His Word is already *now*. Hebrews 11:1 says *now faith is*.

Since the work is finished, we must bring our faith and our prayer into agreement with the Word that what we believe in is already done.

Be the Word!

Since we understand that the work is already done, then we have no need to worry.

> *Now faith is the substance of things hoped for,*
> *the evidence of things not seen.*
>
> Hebrews 11:1 NKJV

The Father does not live in time. He only exists in the now. He is not past or future, but now. Only man lives in time. There is no time in the Kingdom, so all things are now.

Now the blessing of Abraham is resting upon us, but we need to receive and confess it as though it is working in our lives now.

When we confess the Word, we are speaking God's promises—the blessings, life eternal, prosperity, peace, and rest. The reason we do not comprehend this is because we forget that we are the just. Because we are righteous in Christ Jesus, we are already in right standing. All we need to add to this recipe is to be in agreement with the Father and His Word.

We must see ourselves as the sons and daughters of the Living God. The Father's desire is for us to have all the promises He has left us. The only way we can receive them is to believe and speak affirmations of the Word in the *now*.

Be the Word!

When we understand our Father is for us, then we can trust and know that all things are working for our good.

> *"Now someone may argue, 'Some people have faith; others have good deeds.' But I say, 'How can you show me your faith if you don't have good deeds? I will show you my faith by my good deeds.'"*
>
> JAMES 2:18 NLT

My friends, every believer I know has a desire to please their heavenly Father. You do not need works to become a born-again believer, but afterward our faith must begin to grow.

James 2:15 says if we see a brother in need and refuse to help him and say, "We will pray for you" (religion), then our faith is in vain. How many people do you know who sit in church weekly and have vain or dead faith?

Good works accompany faith (Kingdom). Anyone who reads this nugget and does nothing, is like someone who looks in a mirror and then forgets his own face. Have you had a faith check-up lately?

Be the Word!

Your faith is revealed by your actions.

> *Abraham acted in faith when he stood*
> *in the presence of God, who gives life to the dead*
> *and calls into existence things that don't yet exist.*
>
> ROMANS 4:17 ISV

We are citizens of both earth and heaven. We are on the earth, but not of it. That is because the Spirit of God has come from heaven to live within us.

This should make our vocabulary change from the earth realm to Kingdom. That is why the Kingdom tells us to call those things which are not as though they were.

For example, the Kingdom says let the weak (sick) say, "I am strong (healed)." Let the poor say, "I am rich."

In religion, that is a lie, but in the Kingdom, it is true because everything is already finished.

Revelation 13:8 tells us the Lamb of God was slain from the foundation of the world.

Be the Word!

Our Father God gives life to the dead and calls into being that which did not exist, and we are His sons.

> *And [You] have made us kings and priests to our God;*
> *And we shall reign on the earth."*
>
> REVELATION 5:10 NIV

One of the biggest things I see taking place in the body of Christ is that we do not understand who or what we are in the Kingdom of God. We do not know that we are the righteous of the Lord and that we have been redeemed and are sanctified or set apart.

If we comprehend the Kingdom, then we can understand the finished work. All we need to do is to receive what Jesus has already prepared for us.

The Holy Spirit is trying to get us to take our authority on the earth. Jesus said He has put all things under our feet because we have dominion in the earth.

Be the Word!

We have been given the authority to enforce the Word of Truth over the lies of the enemy.

> *That which has been born of the flesh is flesh, and that which has been born of the Spirit is spirit. Do not be amazed that I said to you, 'You must be born again.'*
>
> JOHN 3:6-7 NASB

Religion is man's effort to contact God. It is out of the flesh or the soulish realm. Kingdom is what we are born into when we are born from above.

Jesus told Nicodemus that man's second birth is spiritual, and that's how man is born into the Kingdom. Now, we must study to learn the ways of the Kingdom, which is of and by the Spirit.

Religion walks and lives by head knowledge or man's reasoning. You can only see and enter into the Kingdom by faith. That is why Paul said those who are led by the Spirit of God are the mature ones or the sons of God (Rom. 8:14).

Be the Word!

*Religion is man leading himself.
Kingdom is man led by the Holy Spirit.*

> *"Are you the teacher of Israel, and do not know these things? ... If I have told you earthly things and you do not believe, how will you believe if I tell you heavenly things?"*
>
> JOHN 3:10, 12 NKJV

When Nicodemus approached Jesus and told Him, "We know that you are a teacher who comes from God," he was trying to comprehend the Kingdom with his religious and traditional mindset. This is why Jesus said, "Blessed is the person who hungers and thirsts after righteousness (truth)."

We must hunger for the Kingdom. If not, when we hear the truth, our religious mindset, which walks by our reasoning rather than by the Spirit, will not let us receive or comprehend what the Spirit is saying.

The Kingdom never makes sense to religion because the Kingdom cannot be seen; it must be revealed. It is invisible like faith, the Holy Spirit, and salvation. All of these must be revealed to your spirit.

Be the Word!

The Kingdom cannot be seen but must be revealed.

> *The centurion answered and said, "Lord, I am not worthy that You should come under my roof. But only speak a word, and my servant will be healed. For I also am a man under authority, having soldiers under me. And I say to this one, 'Go,' and he goes; and to another, 'Come,' and he comes; and to my servant, 'Do this,' and he does it."*
>
> Matthew 8:8-9 NKJV

Jesus always preached and talked about the Kingdom. The first sermon He preached was "Repent for the Kingdom of Heaven is at hand."

Most Christians have no understanding of what Kingdom is or what it means. A kingdom is a politically organized community or major territorial unit having a monarchical form of government headed by a king or queen.

Saints, this is what we are a part of. When you understand this, it will revolutionize your life. The centurion soldier understood authority when he asked Jesus to heal his servant and Jesus said He would come to heal him. The soldier said, "I am a man under authority, and I understand that all you need to do is speak the word." He understood that Jesus had Kingdom authority on the earth. So do we.

Be the Word!

We have been translated out of the power of darkness into the Kingdom of God.

> *Everyone then who hears these words of mine*
> *and does them will be like a wise man*
> *who built his house on the rock.*
>
> Matthew 7:24-27 ESV

When you look at our churches, government, the media, and education systems, you can see that our world is in trouble. It starts with the family, then the church and the government, because we are building a foundation on sinking sand.

Jesus said the Kingdom is the rock. Whenever man believes that he is more intelligent than the Bible, we are headed for tragedy and disaster on every level. We have forgotten the first sermon that Jesus preached: "Repent, for the Kingdom of heaven is at hand."

He preached for three and a half years about the Kingdom, not religion. Kingdom is what Jesus died for so we can walk in our authority.

Be the Word!

When we comprehend how authority works,
we will understand the Kingdom of God.

*And have made us kings and priests to our God;
And we shall reign on the earth.*

Revelation 5:10 NKJV

Our society and most of our religious institutions do not understand the Kingdom or know that the Kingdom even exists.

In Jesus' day the religious groups had no clue what He was talking about when He spoke about the Kingdom. His first sermon was repent, change your mind and way of doing things, and first seek the Kingdom.

Jesus came into the earth to establish the dominion or authority that the Lord gave Adam and Adam lost when he and Eve were deceived.

Most people believe that Jesus came to reestablish a religion. Adam never had religion; he had Kingdom.

Be the Word!

The enemy would like to keep us ignorant of who we are: kings, priests, and prophets who have dominion.

> *For to us a child is born, to us a son is given,*
> *and the government will be on his shoulders.*
>
> ISAIAH 9:6 NIV

Kingdom carries authority and power. Jesus came to demonstrate the Kingdom to us. When you look at tradition or religion, you can see there is no power or authority in it.

The Pharisees always debated with Jesus about the things He did. Jesus understood Kingdom government, but they did not. To govern means to rule. When we understand that Kingdom means government, then we can know that we have dominion (Gen. 1:26).

The Lord put us here to rule the earth. The Father gave us the Kingdom (Luke 12:32).

A government prevails and has power over its territory. This is why Jesus told us whatever we permit on earth, heaven will permit, and whatever we bind on earth, heaven will bind (Matt. 18:19).

Be the Word!

Ignorance is our adversary.

> *And [he] hast made us unto our God kings and priests:*
> *and we shall reign on the earth.*
>
> REVELATION 5:10 KJV

The Kingdom of God is made up of certain laws, or principles, which cannot be broken and work every time. What causes an airplane to fly is the law of motion which consists of lift, weight, thrust, and drag. Because man understands this principle, he can command a small aircraft or a jumbo jet to lift off and rest or glide on the air.

Principles work the same in the Kingdom if you comprehend them. Jesus came into His ministry preaching repent or change your direction (change of mind), for the Kingdom of heaven is at hand. This is why the Word tells us that He has made us to be kings and priests in the earth and to have dominion over the earth.

Without understanding Kingdom principles, we cannot function successfully in the Kingdom.

Be the Word!

We are kings and priests, so we should reign on the earth.

For He rescued us from the domain of darkness, and transferred us to the kingdom of His beloved Son.

Colossians 1:13 NASB

Saints, what separates the supernatural from the natural is revelation of the Kingdom. Every born-again believer has the Kingdom in them.

Not having the revelation of the Kingdom is like having a computer without understanding how it works.

The Pharisees had the Law of Moses and quoted and read it daily. They went to synagogue daily and dedicated their life to the Law, but when they saw Jesus demonstrating the Kingdom, they rejected it.

When John's disciples asked Jesus if He was the Messiah or did they need to look for another, He replied, "The lame walk, the blind see, the dumb talk, the deaf hear, and the lepers are cleansed" (Matt. 11:3-5).

That is what the Kingdom looks like in action.

Be the Word!

When you walk in the Kingdom of God, you will do what Jesus did.

Kingsdom Principles

> *From the days of John the Baptist until now*
> *the kingdom of heaven suffers violent assault,*
> *and violent men seize it by force [as a precious prize].*
>
> MATTHEW 11:12 AMP

My friends, if the Kingdom of God is not valuable or precious, then why do violent people attack it? You can see that in Jesus' time it was religious people and the government that came against Him and the Kingdom.

Still today you can see the government enacts laws that are contrary to the Kingdom. You can also see religious people embracing their agenda. This is because they do not comprehend the Kingdom, but religion.

In Jesus' time on earth, He operated by the principles of the Kingdom which call the blind to see, the dumb to speak, the deaf to hear, the lame to walk, and lepers to be cleansed.

Kingdom is demonstrated not in words only but through love, dominion, and power.

The kingdom of heaven suffers violence, and the violent take it by force.

Be the Word!

When we comprehend the Kingdom,
we too will see Kingdom power.

> *But first and most importantly seek (aim at, strive after)
> His kingdom and His righteousness [His way of doing and
> being right—the attitude and character of God],
> and all these things will be given to you also.*
>
> MATTHEW 6:33 AMP

Jesus presented questions about why we worry and don't trust the Father when we can see that He takes care of the birds and flowers, and we know He loves us much more.

Jesus is saying that the things we seek after are the same things that the world seeks. When we do not comprehend Kingdom, we operate as though we are in religion. Religion does not know nor understand Kingdom. Religion believes we will enter into the Kingdom when we go to heaven, but Jesus said in the Lord's prayer, "Thy Kingdom come on earth as it is in heaven."

He said it is the good pleasure of the Father to give us the Kingdom.

Be the Word!

Our second birth brings us into the Kingdom of God.

*Do not be afraid and anxious, little flock,
for it is your Father's good pleasure to give you the kingdom.*

Luke 12:32 AMP

People often question me to find out whether they are in the Kingdom or not. I tell them if you are born again and have accepted Jesus into your heart and understand that you have been born the second time from above (heaven), then you have the Kingdom already in you.

Jesus said it is the good pleasure of the Father to give you the Kingdom. Colossians 1:13 says we have been translated out of the kingdom of satan or darkness into the Kingdom of light.

Now that we have received the Kingdom, we need to gain understanding of how to operate in the Kingdom and to dominate our world or life. Knowledge of the kingdom brings clarity, prosperity, and increase.

Be the Word!

*When you understand the Kingdom,
then you know you have authority in this life.*

> *Let not your heart be troubled;*
> *you believe in God, believe also in Me.*
>
> JOHN 14:1 NKJV

When our heart is troubled, it is saying we do not trust our heavenly Father but believe instead that what we see is true.

We know that the Word tells us to walk by faith and not by sight (2 Cor. 5:7). When we choose to be worried or troubled about anything, in reality we are saying to the Lord that this is too hard or too big for us and for Him too. Fear will cause us to think, talk, and act crazy because of False Evidence Appearing Real.

John 1:1 says that the Word was in the beginning and in the beginning was the Word. So, when we doubt the Word, we are saying that we have more faith in our fear(s) than we have in the Word.

We cannot please God without faith (Hebrews 11:1). Everything we do toward the Kingdom will always be by faith. The key to pleasing the Father is to have faith and trust and enter into His rest.

Be the Word!

Fear always reveals what's in the heart.

*And he arose, and rebuked the wind, and said unto the sea,
Peace, be still. And the wind ceased,
and there was a great calm.*

MARK 4:39 KJV

We can see by example how Jesus operated in the Kingdom. When the storm arose, He commanded it to be still, and peace appeared. The elements obeyed His words.

Blind Bartimaeus asked Jesus to have mercy upon him. Jesus called him and asked, "What do you want me to do for you?" Bartimaeus answered, "That I might receive my sight."

The Word (Jesus) came into agreement with him, saying, "Go your way. Your faith has made you whole."

We must comprehend that the Kingdom is activated by releasing the Word of God out of our mouth.

What's in your mouth?

Be the Word!

*Jesus demonstrated and activated the Kingdom
through the spoken Word.*

> *The mind governed by the flesh is hostile to God;
> it does not submit to God's law, nor can it do so.*
>
> ROMANS 8:7 NIV

My friends, we cannot understand the Kingdom with our natural minds. The carnal mind is contrary to the Kingdom of God. It will lead you against the Kingdom. It will not bring you into agreement with the Word, because things of the Kingdom are spiritually discerned.

Ephesians 2:6 tells us that we have been raised up and made to sit together in heavenly places in Christ Jesus. I have been a Christian for fifty-plus years, and this verse just baffles my mind when I try to comprehend that we are already seated with Christ at the right hand of the Father.

This tells us that we already have victory on every dimension, but it is only revealed to those who hunger and thirst after the Kingdom.

Be the Word!

*Religion looks toward going to heaven,
but we in the Kingdom know we are already seated there.
- Kayla Kennada*

> *Jesus replied, "You are the [great and well-known] teacher of Israel, and yet you do not know nor understand these things [from Scripture]?*
>
> JOHN 3:10 AMP

It grieves me to see so many sincere people who are wrapped up in religion because they lack understanding of the Kingdom.

Understanding the Kingdom brings revelation, insight, power, and authority. When you just have religion, you do not know you have these things.

The Word tells us that God's people are destroyed for the lack of knowledge (Hosea 4:6). When we do not understand Kingdom, then we can read the Bible daily and still be destroyed because we read it with a religious perspective.

Saints, it is critical to ask the Holy Spirit to reveal the Kingdom unto us. Jesus, who demonstrated the Kingdom, said "the blind see, the lame walk, the lepers are cleansed, the deaf hear, the dead are raised, and the poor have the gospel preached to them" (Luke 7:22).

Be the Word!

In the Kingdom of God, the needs of the people are met.

*Blessed are those who hunger and thirst for righteousness,
For they shall be filled.*

Matthew 5: 6 NKJV

Jesus walked and functioned in the earth with the Kingdom perspective. The Pharisees functioned with a religious perspective. They prayed for miracles while Jesus performed them. The Pharisees talked about healing, but Jesus healed. The difference is they prayed for God to heal and work miracles, while Jesus used His authority to heal and bring forth miracles.

We, the body of Christ, should look like and imitate our elder brother Jesus. We talk about walking in the supernatural, but can't walk in it without walking in the Kingdom. We can't walk in the Kingdom if we don't understand it.

Jesus said it is the Father's desire to give us the Kingdom. Jesus taught the Beatitudes (Matt. 5: 3-10). Those are the attributes and blessings that come from walking in the Kingdom.

Be the Word!

*Blessed are they who do the will of God,
for they walk in the Kingdom of God.*

> *The thief comes only to steal and kill and destroy;*
> *I came so that they would have life,*
> *and have it abundantly.*
>
> John 10:10 NASB

It is important for the body of Christ to be Kingdom minded and to understand that our purpose is to have dominion over the earth on every level. It is the Father's will for us to prosper while we are here. If heaven is a place of prosperity, wealth, peace, and harmony, then the Father desires for us to have the same now, here on the earth.

Jesus taught His disciples to pray, "Thy kingdom come on earth as it is in heaven." Jesus said to seek first the Kingdom and then prosperity shall be added unto us. The lack of knowledge of the Kingdom or of prosperity will cause us not to prosper because things come to us through revelation or knowledge of the Word.

A poverty mindset causes us to seek things first rather than the Kingdom. Seeking things first will always lead us to lack and incompleteness.

Be the Word!

Understanding of the Kingdom always produces abundance.

> *In every thing give thanks:*
> *for this is the will of God in Christ Jesus concerning you.*

> 1 THESSALONIANS 5:18 KJV

Let us be thankful for all Jesus has done for us. He became God in the flesh. He taught us how to use the authority and power He has given us. He established the Kingdom, God's government, on the earth.

Isaiah 9:6 tells us that a child is born to us, a son is given to us, and the government will rest on his shoulders. The definition of government is the body of persons that constitutes or makes up the governing authority. We are that body of persons, and Jesus is our governing authority. Now we represent Jesus on the earth. In other words, we are the Kingdom.

When we are thankful for something, we do not take it for granted, but we put it to use. Since it was our Father's good pleasure to give us the kingdom (Luke 12:32), then we know it is Father's will that we walk in it.

Be the Word!

We know the Kingdom is of utmost importance because Jesus spent His life preparing it for us.

Then the shepherds returned, glorifying and praising God for all the things that they had heard and seen, as it was told them.

Luke 2:20 NKJV

The angels revealed the birth of Jesus, the long-awaited Messiah, to the shepherds in the field tending the flocks. The Lord did not tell the religious people, but He showed Himself to the world. King Herod went to the chief priest and the scribes of the church to find out where Jesus was, but they didn't know because tradition, denomination, and religion had blinded them from the truth.

The Lord revealed Himself to those who were hungry and thirsty after Him. The wise men were hungry for the King of the Jews. They traveled a great distance bringing wealth with them for the King of Kings.

Today, Saints, we should do the same. We should hunger and thirst after the Kingdom and bring our gifts to Him. Whatever He has given to us does not belong to us, but to Him.

Be the Word!

The greatest gift we can give to our King is to present ourselves as a living sacrifice unto Him (Rom. 12:2).

> *"I will give you the keys of the kingdom of heaven; and whatever you bind (declare to be improper and unlawful) on earth must be what is already bound in heaven; and whatever you loose (declare lawful) on earth must be what is already loosed in heaven."*
>
> MATTHEW 16:19 AMP

If you can gain understanding of this verse, it will change your life. Jesus said, "I'm going to give you the Kingdom."

The key is your mouth and your words. You are the one who is in authority: man or woman of God, priest, king, prophet, minister, teacher, and saint.

Now take your dominion and rule and reign in the earth as Jesus has shown us time and time again.

He spoke to the storm and commanded it to have peace and be still. He did not talk about the rain, the wind, the water in the boat, the fear, or how big the waves were as we do today. We talk about our president, our pain, our sickness, our sorrow, our fear. We speak what we don't want into existence.

Life is a choice. Choose the Word.

Be the Word!

Everything we say is a choice of life or death.

Nothing in all creation is hidden from God's sight.
Everything is uncovered and laid bare
before the eyes of him to whom we must give account.

HEBREWS 4:13 NIV

What are you going to say when you vote contrary to the Word and then stand before the Lord and the over sixty million aborted babies? My friends, we look like the children of Israel when the Lord told them not to worship other gods and they did it anyway.

Now our nation, churches, pastors, and friends, are walking contrary to the Word of God when they vote or stand in agreement with abortion, euthanasia, homosexuality, and same sex marriage.

Our opinion is not important. What is important is what the Word has spoken concerning these things. What we are looking at is people who are involved in religion but do not understand the Kingdom or what it means to rule or have dominion over the earth or the government.

Do you stand with our culture or the Word?

Be the Word!

In the Kingdom of God, our standard should be the Word.

*And if anyone does not obey our word in this epistle, note that person and do not keep company with him,
that he may be ashamed.*

2 Thessalonians 3:14 NKJV

When we understand the Kingdom and have a relationship and spend time with the Father daily, then our heart's desire is to please the Father rather than our culture, our political party, our denomination, or our family.

When you operate in religion, you do not know the Father or His will and so you are influenced by the worldly culture of Hollywood, news, and pop music. Instead of our schools teaching biblical principles, they teach culture that is contrary to the Word of God.

We can apply the above Scripture verse as a guide when we vote on issues and candidates.

It is critical for the body of Christ to understand that our culture does not know the truth, the Kingdom, or the Word. They are in the dark trying to find the light.

We are the light, so be the light.

Be the Word!

The Kingdom is not measured by Hollywood, opinion polls, culture, or the government, but by God's Word.

For we walk by faith, not by sight.

2 Corinthians 5:7 KJV

The Kingdom is about believing in that which we do not see with our physical eyes. The invisible is more real than the physical.

People say they do not believe in what they cannot see, but they see evidence every day of the law of gravity and the law of lift. They see airplanes soaring through the air and birds gliding on the wind. This is proof of something they cannot see.

Kingdom people walk by the invisible and intangible rather than by the visible or tangible. To do this, we must be able to switch our brain off because it is controlled by the five senses.

Satan deals with the reasoning faculty. The Holy Spirit deals with the spirit man that is the real you. To stay strong in your belief, you must pay more attention to the Kingdom than to the physical world around you.

Be the Word!

We must release the Kingdom that is trapped within us.

6

LED BY THE SPIRIT
Power from on High

*"But you will receive power
when the holy Spirit comes upon you,
and you will be my witnesses in Jerusalem,
throughout Judea and Samaria,
and to the ends of the earth."*

Acts 1:8 NABRE

> *But the Helper (Comforter, Advocate, Intercessor, Counselor, Strengthener, Standby), the Holy Spirit, whom the Father will send in My name [in My place, to represent Me and act on My behalf], He will teach you all things. And He will help you remember everything that I have told you.*
>
> JOHN 14:26 AMP

If we have received the Holy Spirit, and He lives within us, then our greatest quest should be how to release this great power to move in our lives.

We should live by a standard in the body of Christ that is different from the world and from the believers who are not filled with the baptism of the Holy Spirit. His presence within us should cause such a difference that others have a desire or thirst to be like us or to have what we have.

My friends, we should be causing others to thirst for the supernatural.

Be the Word!

When the Holy Spirit makes a difference in your life it should cause you to make a difference in the lives of those around you.

He must become greater; I must become less.

JOHN 3:30 NIV

Too often believers do not understand the role of the Holy Spirit and this great Power we have living in us and with us. The world does not have the Holy Spirit, nor does it know Him. Yet often I do not see any difference between believers who are filled with the Holy Spirit and those who are not.

I challenge the Holy Spirit to help me to be mindful and to be conscious of Him. I tell Him I want and need Him to be Lord of my life. With this power that we have, we should be superheroes to the world and to the body of Christ.

When trouble comes, people need to know that we are in touch with the power from on high. We need to walk more in the Spirit rather than by sight.

Be the Word!

*How can you affect the world today
by releasing the power of the Holy Spirit Who lives in you?*

For I did not receive it from a human being, nor was I taught it, but it came through a revelation of Jesus Christ.

G̲A̲L̲A̲T̲I̲A̲N̲S̲ 1:12 NASB

My friends, we need to spend our time seeking the face of the Holy Spirit to ask Him to reveal the Kingdom to us. Revelation of the Kingdom will transform our whole universe.

If the Word of God is not revealed to us, we can never receive the benefits that come from the Living Word.

Paul said in Galatians that He was more religious than all of his ancestors. He worked hard to destroy the church and all those who called upon the name of Jesus. When he received the revelation of the Kingdom, his world changed forever. He was no longer called Saul, but Paul. With revelation, this man changed the world. Paul said what he received did not come through theology or religion but by revelation from the Holy Spirit.

Be the Word!

Not by might, not by power, but by My Spirit, says the Lord (Zech. 4:6).

"But you will receive power when the Holy Spirit comes on you; and you will be my witnesses in Jerusalem, and in all Judea and Samaria, and to the ends of the earth."

Acts 1:8 NIV

We say that we believe in the Word, but if we do, then we need to have a greater desire for the Holy Spirit to manifest Himself in and through us. We are the people with the power, so there should be a noticeable difference between those of us who are Spirit filled and led and those who are not.

Being a witness means that our family, neighbors, co-workers, and schoolmates can see the anointing of the Lord upon our lives. We must focus to be more conscious of the power that is in and with us.

When trouble comes, the world needs to know where to come to find help because they have seen the witness of your life and know that the Lord is with you by what they have seen you overcome.

The same Spirit that raised Jesus Christ from the dead dwells in us.

Be the Word!

*Remember, greater is He that is in us
than he that is in the world.*

But if the Spirit of Him who raised Jesus from the dead dwells in you, He who raised Christ from the dead will also give life to your mortal bodies through His Spirit who dwells in you.

Romans 8:11 NKJV

I am often asked how a person can demonstrate the power of God that is within them. I tell them to look for opportunities to bridge the gap in the lives of others around them.

Take the opportunity to speak life to someone who is facing a great challenge or lay hands on the afflicted and release healing. In the name of Jesus, command unclean spirits to come out of those who are possessed.

You must remember that you have the same Spirit in you Who raised Jesus from the dead, but you must activate your faith with action for the Spirit's power to manifest.

Peter and John went to the temple, and the crippled man asked them for alms. They commanded him to rise and walk in the name of Jesus, but they activated their faith when they reached down and grabbed him by the hand and stood him up.

Always remember that real faith requires action.

Be the Word!

People who have faith take action.

> *As a result, people brought the sick into the streets and laid them on beds and mats so that at least Peter's shadow might fall on some of them as he passed by.*
>
> ACTS 5:15 NIV

After the day of Pentecost, there was a tangible difference in the lives of the disciples. They went from being cowards to becoming martyrs. My God, my Lord, what a change!

Can you or anyone else tell the difference in you since you received the baptism of the Holy Spirit? Remember, receiving Jesus gives us authority, and receiving the Holy Spirit gives us *dunamis* power.

If the disciples cast out demons before they received the baptism of the Holy Spirit, how much more should we be doing with the baptism of the Holy Spirit?

Saints, it is not enough for me to just go to church on Sundays or to say I am a Christian or speak with other tongues. I desire for the power of God Who abides in me to explode upon the circumstances around me. When you have the power of the Holy Spirit operating through you, people will come to you to seek the anointing that abides in you.

Be the Word!

It should be a way of life to continually release the power of the Holy Spirit that is within you.

For it is not you who speak,
but the Spirit of your Father who speaks in you.

MATTHEW 10:20 NKJV

Saints, we must look for opportunities to release the power of the Holy Spirit Who dwells in us. We must bridge the gap for people who are overcoming sickness and give the Holy Spirit an opportunity to show Himself strong on the earth.

I go to different churches to minister, and if I say we are going to have a healing service, healing manifests. If I say we will have a prophecy service, then prophecies go forth. If I say nothing, then the Holy Spirit's presence is not noticeable.

We must give the Holy Spirit an opportunity to work in and through us. It is important for us to understand that we are the temple of the Holy Spirit. We are His voice, hands, and feet. The Spirit of God is trapped on the inside of us when we do not release Him. If we release Him, then others will be set free from their bondage.

Be the Word!

The Holy Spirit can only work through us
when we release Him and allow Him to operate through us.

*You know of Jesus of Nazareth, how God anointed Him
with the Holy Spirit and with power,
and how He went about doing good
and healing all who were oppressed by the devil,
for God was with Him.*

Acts 10:38 NASB

We tend to forget that we are the temple of the Holy Spirit. Sometimes we try to send the Holy Spirit to do this or that for us, but unless we go, He cannot go, because we are His voice, hands, and feet. The Spirit of God travels with and in us.

Jesus had to go in order for people to be healed. We think we just have to sit at home and pray. Just as the Father used Jesus to go to heal the sick and oppressed, He wants to do the same today in and through us.

Saints, we must go, as Jesus said, into all the earth.

Be the Word!

Do not be like the world, be the Word!

> *Peter replied, "Repent and be baptized, every one of you, in the name of Jesus Christ for the forgiveness of your sins. And you will receive the gift of the Holy Spirit. The promise is for you and your children and for all who are far off—for all whom the Lord our God will call."*
>
> ACTS 2:38-39 NIV

Jesus told His disciples to go tarry in the upper room until they received power. They received the infilling of the Holy Spirit with power, and the evidence was that they spoke in other tongues. Those 120 disciples' lives were changed forever.

Peter was a coward when he was asked if he knew Jesus. He denied Him three times just as the Lord said he would, and even cussed, because he was afraid for his life. He had been with Jesus for three and a half years yet did not have much power or authority until he received the baptism of the Holy Spirit. After he received the Holy Spirit with power, Peter stood and preached and three thousand were saved. He preached again, and five thousand gave their lives to the Lord (Acts 4:4).

What a difference the Holy Spirit makes in a person's life!

Be the Word!

How does the power of the Holy Spirit manifest in your daily life?

> *He said to them, "Did you receive the holy Spirit
> when you became believers?" They answered him,
> "We have never even heard that there is a holy Spirit."*
>
> Acts 19:2 NABRE

My friends, what love the Father has for us, His children. John 14:26 AMP says He will send the Helper (Comforter, Advocate, Intercessor, Counselor, Strengthener, Standby), the Holy Spirit. This is the same power or Spirit that empowered Jesus Christ, the Son of the Living God.

The Word tells us the same Spirit that raised Christ from the dead lives and dwells in us also. This power is the Comforter the Father promised us. This is why the Word of God tells us we can do all things through Christ.

We have been chosen for such a work and for such a time as this. One of the last commandments Jesus gave His disciples was to go into Jerusalem and wait until they received power from heaven (Luke 24:49).

This power from heaven lives within you now. Release the power that is within.

Be the Word!

*The Holy Spirit dwells in us with power,
but it is up to us to release that power.*

> *For our struggle is not against flesh and blood,*
> *but against the rulers, against the authorities,*
> *against the powers of this dark world*
> *and against the spiritual forces of evil in the heavenly realms.*
>
> Ephesians 6:12 NIV

The Word of God tells us we are not wrestling against flesh and blood, but against principalities, powers, and rulers of darkness. This is why the Father has given us the Comforter, the Holy Spirit Himself. Jesus told the 120 disciples to go to the Upper Room to wait for power from on high.

Saints, in order to deal with principalities, we must have power. If we understand how the Holy Spirit works in and through us, we can have more confidence in ourselves and also in the Word.

The Holy Spirit lives with power in our spirit. The Word comes alive in our spirit when we release the Holy Spirit to pray in and through us.

We can change many outcomes in our daily lives by praying in the Holy Spirit or in tongues. That is our key to power and success.

Be the Word!

We have the power to change circumstances in this world by praying in the Holy Spirit.

> *"He must become greater; I must become less."*
>
> JOHN 3:30 NIV

Saints, too often believers do not understand the role of the Holy Spirit and this great power that we have living in us and with us. The world does not have the Holy Spirit, nor does it know Him. Yet much of the time, I really do not see any difference between those filled with the Holy Spirit and those who are not.

I challenge the Holy Spirit to help me to be mindful and conscious of Him. I tell Him I want and need for Him to be Lord of my life.

With this power we possess, we should be superheroes to the world and to the body of Christ. When trouble comes, people need to know that we are people who are in touch with the power from on high. We need to walk more in the Spirit rather than by sight. We must decrease so He can increase.

Be the Word!

How can you affect the world today by releasing the power of the Holy Spirit within you?

7

THE POWER OF THE WORD
Living and Effective

*Indeed, the word of God is living and effective,
sharper than any two-edged sword,
penetrating even between soul and spirit,
joints and marrow, and able to discern
reflections and thoughts of the heart.*

Hebrews 4:12 NABRE

> *Indeed, the word of God is living and effective, sharper than any two-edged sword, penetrating even between soul and spirit, joints and marrow, and able to discern reflections and thoughts of the heart.*
>
> HEBREWS 4:12 NABRE

The Word can tell the difference between our soul and spirit and joints and marrow and expose our thoughts and purpose of our heart. That alone is mind boggling, but the Word does so much more for us.

The Word is a lamp to our feet and a light to our path. It enables us to prosper. It is our source of victory to overcome all situations of life. The Word is the way, the truth, and the life for us. And this is just a portion of what the Word can do.

Our lives can be so much better if we put the Word to use. It can't do anything for us unless we release it to go to work on our behalf.

The Lord has already given us everything we need for life and godliness (2 Peter 1:3). So, if you lack anything or any area, it is not His fault. He has already supplied all of our needs. It is up to us to activate the Word and receive all He has for us.

Be the Word!

He sent His word and healed them and delivered them from their destruction (Ps. 107:20).

The Power of the Word

Therefore we do not become discouraged (utterly spiritless, exhausted, and wearied out through fear). Though our outer man is [progressively] decaying and wasting away, yet our inner self is being [progressively] renewed day after day.

2 Corinthians 4:16 AMP

What I want you to comprehend is that your spirit man never dies. He is being renewed daily by the confession of your words. All the power is in your spirit.

When we read, speak, meditate, pray, and talk about the Word, the inner man gets stronger and stronger every day.

The outer man you see in the mirror is not the real you. Everything that deals with the real you, such as faith, is all in the spirit realm.

Jesus said that words are spirits (John 6:63).

Be the Word!

The only thing that makes our spiritual man strong is the Word.

> *But be doers of the word, and not hearers only, deceiving yourselves.*
>
> JAMES 1:22 NKJV

Having faith means taking action toward what you believe. When you believe in something, you will act on it. When you believe the Word, it will work for you.

For example, the Word tells us to bring the entire tithe into the storehouse. When you have faith in this Word, you will take action by doing what the Word says to do, which in this case is to bring your tithe to the place where you are ministered to or fed the Word of God. When you take this action, the Word says the Lord Himself will rebuke the devourer for your sake.

Trust the Lord by giving Him a tenth, and He will cause you to prosper in every aspect of life.

There is always a reward when you put action to your faith in the Word of God.

Be the Word!

When we trust the Lord and His Word, then we can believe and receive.

But someone will say, "You have faith, and I have works."
Show me your faith without your works,
and I will show you my faith by my works.

JAMES 2:1 NKJV

Many times, people hear me preach and teach and then come away thinking I am bitter or angry because of the passion I have for revelation of the truth.

I can see religion and tradition blinding the minds of God's people because they believe they are waiting upon the Lord to answer their prayer or to heal them or fix a situation in their life. They don't understand that along with their belief, they must take a step of faith in order to change their situation.

Believing the Word is not enough. Every Christian is a believer, but look at our circumstances. Without faith, Saints, we will be defeated while holding the Bible in our hands and sitting in the pews three times a week.

James says show me your faith by your works. It takes believing and faith with action.

Be the Word!

When you have faith in the Word,
you will be a doer of the Word.

> *So shall my word be that goes forth from my mouth;*
> *It shall not return to me empty, but shall do what pleases me,*
> *achieving the end for which I sent it.*
>
> Isaiah 55:11 NABRE

When I look at the goodness in my life, sometimes I could just cry thinking about all the things I have overcome by the power of understanding how to speak the Word over my life. This is why Bridging the Gap always talks about being the Word, speaking the Word, and praying the Word, because it is the Word that brings life or change to our circumstances.

I discovered that the Bible works if we work it. What I mean is if we are in agreement with the Word of God by releasing it out of our mouth and spending time daily meditating the Word, it will perform in our lives every time. I praise my Lord and my Savior for opening my understanding to the power of confessing the Word over sickness, poverty, and fear.

Isaiah said the Word of the Lord shall not return unto Him void or empty. This truth only works if you apply the Word by speaking it with your lips.

Be the Word!

You see the goodness of the Lord in the land of the living by agreeing with and speaking His Word.

The Power of the Word

For verily I say unto you, Till heaven and earth pass, one jot or one tittle shall in no wise pass from the law, till all be fulfilled.

Matthew 5:18 KJV

Friends, many times in life I can see the mountains to my left and to my right. I even see a mountain behind me in my rearview mirror. I always have this confidence within me that it is impossible for the Word to lie.

Jesus said until heaven and earth pass away, even the tiniest letter of the law will remain until all is fulfilled. The Lord said this to us because He wants us to have confidence in His Word.

We know from John 1:14 that the Word itself stepped out of the spiritual realm into the flesh.

If we can find the promise or blessing in the Word that applies to us or our situation, then we can take that Word and come into agreement with it by declaring what it says several times a day to us and over us.

It is the Word that gives us confidence because we know It existed in the beginning.

Be the Word!

The Word is our constant assurance of victory in our lives.

> *The Lord is my light and my salvation—whom shall I fear?*
> *The Lord is the stronghold of my life—of whom shall I be afraid?*
>
> PSALM 27:1 NIV

If I could know only one chapter in the Bible, it would be Psalm 27. If I could know only one verse, it would be verse one. If I could take only one phrase out of that verse, it would be *the Lord is my salvation*.

The word *salvation* means victory, deliverance, freedom, eternal life, righteousness, sanctification, justification, health, redemption, and wealth.

If we meditate on Psalm 27, we see *the Lord is my light*. This means revelation, enlightenment, clarity, and unveiled. Once we understand this, then we can lean upon and trust the Lord in the storm, darkness, and sickness because we know He has revealed the truth to us. We must come into agreement with the Word and say what it says, believe it, and hide it in our hearts.

My friends, we read the Word but do not comprehend it. Hosea 4:6 says God's people are destroyed for lack of knowledge.

Be the Word!

By the truth of His Word, we are free and delivered.

The Power of the Word

> *I will bless the Lord at all times;*
> *His praise shall continually be in my mouth.*

Psalm 34:1 NKJV

My friends, when we find ourselves in the storms of life we must have the same confidence in the Word in the storm as we do on a sunny day sitting in church. The Word of God never changes regardless of our circumstances.

The apostle Paul was a prisoner on a ship on his way to prison again for preaching the Gospel. He was not discouraged by the shackles that bound him or the storm he found himself in. He was the commander of the ship of over 276 people; yet was not the captain, but a prisoner.

What made the difference with Paul is that he had confidence because he had a relationship with the Father. Acts 27:35-36 states that Paul gave thanks to God in front of all on the ship and everyone was encouraged and began to eat. When you have confidence in the Word then you can give the Father praise in the midst of the storm.

Be the Word!

The storms of life never cause the Word of God to change.

> *So then faith comes by hearing,*
> *and hearing by the word of God.*
>
> Romans 10:17 NKJV

Many times, people do not understand the importance of the words of their mouth which either bring life or death, health or sickness, poverty or prosperity, and peace or chaos. Words are like a time capsule that is going to come to pass in our future.

We must be careful to understand that we are made in the likeness and the image of our heavenly Father. The words of God bring faith. Most Christians do not have faith because they do not speak the Word. Our confession of faith brings us eternal life. Our words will bring us whatever we say and believe.

We must not lose control of our words when we are angry because it will cause us to say things about ourselves or others that are not according to the Word. This is why the Lord told Joshua to ponder the Word both day and night.

Be the Word!

We employ angels when we speak the Word of God.

The Power of the Word

In the beginning was the Word,
and the Word was with God, and the Word was God.

John 1:1 KJV

Faith comes only through the spoken Word, which must be revealed by the Holy Spirit. If it is not revealed to us, then it is like eating a full course meal, but the food never digests in our stomachs. It will not do us any good. It may taste good, but it cannot help us because the nutrition never went into our organs (spirits).

The Bible tells us that in the beginning was the Word, and everything that is and was came through the Word—the spoken Word.

Your life is the fruit of the words spoken from your mouth. Paul says faith can only come to us from hearing and by hearing God's Word. Whose words are you listening to?

Isaiah said that the words of the Lord shall not return unto Him void or empty, but His Word shall accomplish what He sent it to do. The Word must be believed and spoken.

Be the Word!

Everything you see and can't see was spoken into existence
by the Father who created you to be like Him.

> *You are snared by the words of your mouth;*
> *You are taken by the words of your mouth.*
>
> Proverbs 6:2 NKJV

You always hear me speak about the spoken Word of God. I cannot tell you the close calls that we have experienced in our lives as a family or minister of the Gospel. We have seen so many things that should have been tragedy, but were not, because of speaking the Word.

We are snared or taken by what we say. Our words put us in a prison, or they bring us salvation. Our words must be in agreement with the Bible.

When I look at the lives of my children, the fruit of my marriage and ministry, the key to success is speaking the Word in season and out of season.

When you are in pain and when you feel good, when there is no money in your hand or thousands of dollars in your account, you must speak the words of the Bible and what it says about your circumstances. The Word will work every time if you take the time to work the Word.

Be the Word!

You must speak the Word to activate it and bring it from the pages of the Bible into your life and circumstances.

The Power of the Word

Jesus said to him, "[You say to Me,] 'If You can?' All things are possible for the one who believes and trusts [in Me]!"

MARK 9:23 AMP

The Word of God is so simple, yet we cause it to be so complicated with our traditions. The enemy wants to complicate the Word because he does not want us to receive what the Word has for us.

The Lord did not put us here to live a defeated life. He placed us on the earth to walk in victory and authority every day. We must work with the authority He has given us in order for it to work.

Many times, we walk contrary to the Truth. We get frustrated with life, ourselves, the Lord, and anyone else who tries to help us. We must bring our confession and our thoughts into agreement with the Word. Prayer will not work for us if we go against the Word.

Jesus has already died for us. There is nothing else in this world that He has not already taken care of or done for us. All things are possible for those who believe.

Be the Word!

The most common way people give up their power is by thinking they don't have any. – Alice Walker

> *"As for what was sown on good soil, this is he who hears the Word and grasps and comprehends it; he indeed bears fruit and yields in one case a hundred times as much as was sown, in another sixty times as much, and in another thirty."*
>
> MATTHEW 13:23 AMP

In this verse, we can see how important it is that with all of our getting, to get understanding. The Word lets us know that we can only reap what we understand.

This is why Hosea tells us that God's people are destroyed because of the lack of knowledge or understanding and why the Father gave us the Holy Spirit, to teach us how to understand the Word.

Only the Holy Spirit brings revelation. We must put Him first in all things that we do. How can we lose with a teacher and a counselor sent from above to live in us and with us, and to lead us and to guide us into all Truth.

Be the Word!

Is the Holy Spirit your teacher?

> *"This is the covenant I will make with them after that time, says the Lord. I will put my laws in their hearts, and I will write them on their minds."*
>
> Hebrews 10:16 NIV

When we have confidence in the Word, we have confidence in our Father. The Father and His Word are one and the same.

When we read the Bible, we must realize it is our heavenly Father talking to us. We know that He will never lie to us about anything, for it is impossible for Him to lie.

When we have a revelation of this, it will make our faith go to another level. This is what causes us to have confidence. Our confidence is in the Word. Jesus said He put His Word above His name. The Father is bound by His Word.

Be the Word!

*We cannot have the Word and
not have the Father and His benefits.*

> *"I will give you the keys of the kingdom of heaven; and whatever you bind (declare to be improper and unlawful) on earth must be what is already bound in heaven; and whatever you loose (declare lawful) on earth must be what is already loosed in heaven."*
>
> MATTHEW 16:19 AMP

My friends, when you comprehend the magnitude of what Jesus said here to the disciples, it is mind altering. Jesus gave us this example when He walked the earth. He called the dead forth, and He told those who were blind to see.

He is our example for us to imitate in our everyday life. He is telling us to call forth whatever we lack in our life in the natural world. We are to command for our home, marriage, health, family, finances, job, peace, and clarity to come to us.

Speak the answer, not the situation. Angels in heaven are waiting for your words. Speak the Word.

Be the Word!

Since angels listen to perform the spoken word, are you keeping your angels busy?

The Power of the Word

"It is the spirit that gives life, while the flesh is of no avail. The words I have spoken to you are spirit and life."

JOHN 6:63 NASB

That is a powerful statement. Our words are spirits. Every time we release words out of our mouth, a spirit goes forth from us to accomplish what we have spoken and return back to our spirit.

Proverbs 18:21 NCV says it this way: "What you say can mean life or death. Those who speak with care will be rewarded."

We will be rewarded by our words, not the words of others. Our blessing comes from the right words from our own lips. When we understand the power of words, we will be able to comprehend what Romans 10:17 says, that "faith comes by hearing and by hearing the Word of God."

Jesus said His words came to bring us life, health, peace, and prosperity, so these words must be coming from our lips also.

Be the Word!

It's important to remember that words are spirit. Choose your words carefully.

*In the beginning was the Word,
and the Word was with God,
and the Word was God.*

JOHN 1:1 KJV

I can't tell you how important it is to step back from religion and tradition and look at the Word of God. The Word of God is living, powerful, and sharper than a two-edged sword. It deals with every part of man: the spirit, soul, and body.

When I talk about speaking the Word, many hear me, but they don't always comprehend the magnitude of what the Word will do for them if they will speak and agree with it.

Do you understand that the Word is eternal? The Word is God, and God is the Word.

John 1:1 tells us that from the beginning, the disciples heard and saw with their eyes and touched the Word of life with their hands. The Word manifested itself.

My desire is to help you understand the importance of activating the power of the Word in your life.

Be the Word!

*Release the Word from your lips,
and it will manifest in your circumstances.*

The Power of the Word

The Word became flesh and made his dwelling among us. We have seen his glory, the glory of the one and only Son, who came from the Father, full of grace and truth.

JOHN 1:14 NIV

The Word Himself stepped out of the invisible into the visible and walked the earth among flesh and blood men. It is mind boggling.

John 1:1 says the Word was with God in the beginning and the Word is God. What a word! When we release this Word from our lips, we release Christ, the Word.

My friends, this is the purpose and reason the enemy does not want us to speak or understand the Word of life. When you combine the Word with faith, you create a dunamis experience that is able to raise the dead, heal the sick, open blind eyes, and hush the mouths of hurricanes.

This Word lives in us.

Be the Word!

We must release this Word—speak it out— for it to have an effect upon our circumstances.

8

PURPOSE
For Such a Time as This

*For it is God who works in you
to will and to act
in order to fulfill his good purpose.*

Philippians 2:13 NIV

Let us run with endurance the race that is set before us.

Hebrews 12:1 NKJV

We often grow weary running the race of life. Or maybe we come to the realization that we are trying to run the race God gave to someone else to run.

Then, there are those who try to fulfill what the Lord called them to do twenty-five years ago and that season has come to an end. The Lord has more for them to do, but they are stuck in the past.

Doing the right thing at the wrong time can cause frustration, weariness, and even burnout. Remember, it is not important what the Lord told you ten years ago, five years ago, or even a month ago. What did the Holy Spirit say to you today?

Be the Word!

Being led by the Holy Spirit each day is paramount.

> *To everything there is a season,*
> *A time for every purpose under heaven.*
>
> ECCLESIASTES 3:1 NKJV

If our blessings are not flowing, it is because we are not moving with the Holy Spirit. Sometimes we stay too long where He placed us in the past.

The Lord told Abraham to sacrifice Isaac. Abraham proceeded to obey God. After three days of traveling, he and his son came to the place of sacrifice. Then the Lord spoke to Abraham and said, "Do the lad no harm."

We need to listen for a fresh word daily. The Lord gave the Israelites fresh manna on a daily basis. Jesus taught us to pray for our daily bread. Too often we are busy doing what the Lord told us to do, but its season has passed.

Saints, frustration comes when we don't recognize what season we are in. Stay in touch with the Holy Spirit to guide you.

Be the Word!

Seize the season you are in now.

Did you not know that I must be about My Father's business?"

LUKE 2:49 NKJV

All of my life, I have had a concern, and sometimes even a fear, of living life in vain and never fulfilling the purpose for which God created me. I am always concerned about doing and being what the Lord desires me to be.

In the Word, I read that God has set a race before us, and in Ephesians it says that He has ordained a path for us from the foundation of time. Over and over again, the Word tells us everything was prearranged for us.

I struggle to make sure that I do not get caught up in everyday hustle and bustle. At the end of my day, I lie down asking myself what I have done to advance the Kingdom.

When Jesus was on the earth, He always talked about being about His Father's business. Can I ask you a personal question? What are you concerned about? Your Father's business? Or are you caught up in everyday drama?

Be the Word!

If we take care of the Kingdom, it will take care of us.

> *For ye are bought with a price: therefore glorify God in your body, and in your spirit, which are God's.*
>
> 1 CORINTHIANS 6:20 KJV

Many times, when we read the Word of God and look at the history of the Bible and read about the patriarchs, Abraham, Joseph, Samson, David, Esther, Rahab, and Deborah, we imagine what we would have done if we had lived during that time.

I want to ask you a question: What are you doing with your time now? Will history remember you? What will history say about you? Without your tombstone, will the world beyond your grandchildren even know that you existed?

We are writing history now, today, at this moment. What are we doing to change or affect other people's lives?

Our purpose on earth is to work with the Father. Paul said we are co-laborers with God (1 Cor. 3:9). What is your labor? What are you doing? Whose life have you changed for good?

Be the Word!

Our purpose on the earth is to fulfill our Father's purpose.

For we are God's masterpiece. He has created us anew in Christ Jesus, so we can do the good things he planned for us long ago.

EPHESIANS 2:10 NLT

Do you ever think about the patriarchs in the Bible? Many times, I hear people talk negatively about Solomon, the wisest man on the earth. Maybe if he'd had Jesus or the Word of God or a church to be a part of or if he'd understood the Kingdom, then his life and world would have been better.

Though he was the wisest man who ever lived, he did not have God living in Him as we do. He may not have made the mistakes he made if he'd had access to what we take for granted.

My point is that we have church, the Bible, Jesus, and the Holy Spirit. What are we doing with what we have today? Will history call you wise, prosperous, a game changer, or a person of faith? We must remember that we have been ordained for good works. We have greatness in us, and we must pursue the call of the Father.

Be the Word!

What have you done with the dash on your tombstone between the cradle and the grave?

> *He has saved us and called us to a holy life—*
> *not because of anything we have done*
> *but because of his own purpose and grace.*
>
> 2 Timothy 1:9 NIV

How many Christians actually fulfill the purpose for which they were created? I can tell you in my experience as a pastor and a spiritual coach for many years, that most people seek their own plan for their life. Most do not seek first the Kingdom of God as Jesus instructed in Matthew 6:33.

So then, how can the Lord tell them at the end of their life, "Well done" if they did not do what He said for them to do? We are not just called to be saved, but we are called according to His purpose.

Be the Word!

We have to discover our purpose because it is born within us.

> *For I know the plans I have for you," declares the Lord,*
> *"plans to prosper you and not to harm you,*
> *plans to give you hope and a future."*
>
> JEREMIAH 29:11 NIV

My friends, the Lord promised to bring the children of Israel into a land that flowed with milk and honey. He even told them not to forget about Him when they got their silver, gold, land, and houses; yet they never possessed the land of Canaan they were promised even though He said He would do it.

Many times, we see and read about the blessings in the Bible but never possess them because we do not work with the Word of God in order to receive them. We just expect it to happen because it is in the Word. We must work with the Word rather than against it if we are going to inherit the blessings promised to us.

The children of Israel spent their time murmuring and complaining against the Word and never came into agreement with it. We must agree with the Word by meditating on it and speaking affirmations that agree with it, in order to receive the benefits of the Word.

Be the Word!

Our purpose on the earth is to fulfill the Father's purpose.

Therefore, since we are surrounded by so great a cloud of witnesses, let us rid ourselves of every burden and sin that clings to us and persevere in running the race that lies before us.

Hebrews 12:1 NABRE

The Lord has set a race before us, and we are to run it with patience and endurance.

When we come into this world, we do not choose our color, nationality, parents, country, or language. The Lord chose it for us. He has placed us on this earth at this time and season because we are the answers to the troubles our generation is facing. This is our time to be effective in our culture.

If each person would rise up and use what the Father has put in him or her, we could help bring peace to the society we live in.

The Word tells us we are the salt of the earth. We are the light of the world. The world has no light, but we do. Be the light.

Be the Word!

We put our light on the candle stand; we do not hide it under a bushel basket.

Let each person lead the life that the Lord has assigned to him, and to which God has called him.

1 Corinthians 7:17-24 ESV

Our purpose has already been pre-arranged from the foundation of the world. This gives me courage that the Lord has already given us victory from the beginning to the end. Now, all we have to do is trust, believe, and walk therein.

When we learn about trusting our heavenly Father, then we can understand why He tells us not to worry. What He is saying in our terms is "I've got this."

We need to continue to get up every day, put one foot in front of the other, and listen to the Holy Spirit. What the Father has ordained for us will come to pass if we seek what the Holy Spirit wants us to do each day.

Ephesians 2:10 AMP tells us the Lord has already prearranged a good, prosperous, and healthy life for us. Prearranged means it is already fixed. We need to fix our affirmations to be in alignment with the Word.

Be the Word!

If you do not believe the Bible, then what do you believe?

The people who know their God shall be strong, and carry out great exploits.

DANIEL IN 11:32 NKJV

My friends, this is why it is so important for us to develop a relationship with the Father so we can know and be able to discern His voice as He speaks to us to lead, guide, and direct us in the path He wants us to take daily.

There are many people in the Kingdom who are doing work for the Kingdom, but their time and season has come and gone. The Lord wants us to trust Him daily for a fresh word.

Jesus taught His disciples to pray, "Father give us our daily bread, manna in the wilderness, just enough for today."

The Holy Spirit is going to do fresh work in you. So take your hands off the wheel, let Him drive, and you will thrive.

Be the Word!

*The Word tells us to pray, believe, and receive.
You've got this.*

And we know that all things work together for good to those who love God, to those who are the called according to His purpose.

Romans 8:28 NKJV

When the Word says in James 2 to be a doer of the Word and not a hearer only, it is telling us not to just read or study the Word, but to apply it to our lives. This means we are to do more than sit in the pews at church or watch sermons online or on TV. This means we are to get out of our recliners and be the hands and feet of Jesus.

Religion makes us comfortable and self-satisfied. Where is our compassion for those who are hurting, sick, or lost? Too often, we are only concerned about ourselves and our families.

Saints, as the body of Christ, we were called for His purpose. His purpose is to establish the Kingdom of God on earth. His purpose is to seek and save the lost. His purpose is for us to be equipped to do the work of ministry and to edify the body of Christ.

Be the Word!

To be a doer of the Word means to be the Word!

Are you willing to be shown [proof], you foolish (unproductive, spiritually deficient) fellow, that faith apart from [good] works is inactive and ineffective and worthless?

JAMES 2:20 AMP

That's a good definition of someone stuck in religion. If every mature Christian would take time to mentor, disciple, and minister to those around them, we would not have enough room in our churches to hold all the harvest.

If we don't sow love, then we can't reap love. The world cannot love because they don't know the Father. The Word tells us that the Father is love.

If we are mature, we will take the time to seek the Holy Spirit about whom we are supposed to help. Our schools, communities, government, and prisons, will change because we have the truth and the Word.

We are the light, and the world is walking in darkness while Christians are asleep in religion. Let's wake up.

Be the Word!

*Jesus said go into all the world
and preach the gospel to everyone.*

> "Go then and make disciples of all the nations [help the people to learn of Me, believe in Me, and obey My words], baptizing them into the name of the Father and of the Son and of the Holy Spirit."
>
> MATTHEW 28:19 AMP

Saints, do you ever think about what the Word really says? Jesus took twelve men and started a college, a church, social media, wrote songs, and books—oops, not!

Instead of doing all of those things, He taught them the Word and changed the world.

What would happen to our homes, communities, churches, schools, jails, and prisons, and our government if we took time to mentor or disciple people? Can you see how the Kingdom would be able to invade the earth?

The Word tells us we are supposed to imitate Jesus. Jesus made disciples.

Be the Word

Your life may be the only Word that people ever read.

For by grace you have been saved through faith and that not of yourselves; it is the gift of God ... For we are His workmanship, created in Christ Jesus for good works, which God prepared beforehand that we should walk in them.

Ephesians 2:8,10 NKJV

The kingdom of God operates by faith. By faith we are justified and made righteous, and by faith we are sanctified and set apart for the Father's work.

Saints, it is an awesome thing to be chosen by and set apart for a work God has ordained for us from the foundation of the world. It should make us feel special to know that the Word tells us He chose us.

Jesus said, "No man can come to me except the Father draws him." We should be so grateful that the Spirit of the Lord tugged at our spirits, and we answered the call of our eternal Father. We are chosen and ordained for a work that will echo throughout all eternity.

Remember, we were never chosen to do work for ourselves; we are chosen to do work for each other. Our mission is to help each other return home.

Be the Word!

Everything you do for the Lord has eternal significance, so do it all for Him.

About the Author

A prophet and visionary, Dr. Johnnie Blount is known internationally for his ability to guide individuals to spiritual maturity and revelation of the Kingdom of God. He is a dynamic speaker and author who shares the message of the Kingdom Jesus came to reveal. Flowing in the gifts of the Holy Spirit, he serves others by ministering the power, love, grace, and truth in the Word of God.

Dr. Blount's mission is to empower the believer to walk in the possibilities, purpose, provision, and revelation of Kingdom principles.

To accomplish this vision, he founded Bridging the Gap Ministries and Be the Word Kingdom Academy. He writes, speaks, holds conferences, has a weekly online Bible study, and travels throughout the United States as well as internationally.

Dr. Johnnie Blount has been ministering since he was fifteen years old. Throughout his many years of ministry, he has been a pastor, established three churches and two Bible colleges, and has led many mission trips. In ministering to the youth in Job Corps, he and his team led over 15,000 souls to salvation.

Dr. Johnnie and his wife, Donnis, have been married since 1980 and have four children and eight grandchildren and counting.

Dr. Blount can be contacted through his website: https://drjohnnieblount.com

www.ingramcontent.com/pod-product-compliance
Lightning Source LLC
Chambersburg PA
CBHW070737020526
44118CB00035B/1455